# A PHOTOGRAPHIC GUIDE TO
# STABLE MANAGEMENT

# A PHOTOGRAPHIC GUIDE TO
# STABLE
# MANAGEMENT

Expert advice on every aspect of horse care and management
from one of the world's most eminent judges and showmen

## ROBERT OLIVER
### PHOTOGRAPHS BY BOB LANGRISH

d&c

David & Charles

*To quote Whyte-Melville, 'the best of my fun I owe it to horse and hound', and, in my case, to the Ledbury Foxhounds in particular. My grateful thanks to Anna Sturgeon, my secretary and groom, for all her help on the word processor during the writing of this book.*

A DAVID & CHARLES BOOK

Copyright © Robert Oliver 1994

First published 1994

Robert Oliver has asserted his right to be identified as author of this work in accordance with the Copyright, Designs and Patents Act 1988.

A catalogue record for this book is available from the British Library.

ISBN 0 7153 0084 9

Typeset by ABM Typographics Ltd Hull
and printed in Italy by Milanostampa SpA
for David & Charles
Brunel House Newton Aboot Devon

# CONTENTS

Introduction 7

1 Stabling 9

2 Fields and Fencing 37

3 Tack and Clothing 53

4 Feeding 77

5 Grooming and Clipping 91

6 Exercising and Fitness 113

7 Veterinary Care and Shoeing 127

8 Transport 139

Index 149

# INTRODUCTION

My overwhelming intention in writing this book is to help all those who wish to know more about the care and management of horses and ponies in general. Whether student or showman, the standard of care should be the highest you can attain – and as everyone knows, with animals you never stop learning! I have a lifetime's experience on which to draw, starting with one Welsh pony to now running a top professional yard, and I hope that in these pages I have given the reader enough of my knowledge to help him to a more thorough understanding of what is required in the keeping of horses and ponies both stabled and at grass.

There are many right, wrong and different ways to do the same job. The horse is a noble creature, and it is surely the wish of all those who are responsible for him to do as much as possible towards his everyday care. I have tried to cover all the main aspects of horse management, and so sincerely hope that this book will meet a popular need.

They say that every picture tells a story, and that every story is worth a thousand words: the photographs carefully assembled within these pages will provide a pictorial guide to young and old for many years to come. Students as well as those already experienced in the management of horses will surely find points which are new, interesting and relevant in this book. And remember that a well-run, happy yard is always a successful one in every equestrian sphere! Today there are so many books on horses, but I hope you will find in this one the down-to-earth, practical information that you need whatever your standard. Sadly we no longer have the old-fashioned stud groom, always a mine of information on all aspects of horse management; but I hope that in this book I have managed to convey to you all the knowledge taught to me by the old grooms I have known, and which I have found invaluable.

# 1
# STABLING

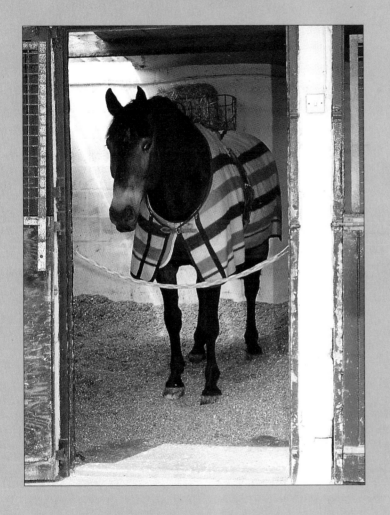

**Stable Design 11**
**Ventilation 17**
**Stable Fitments 18**
**General Standards 23**
**Bedding Materials 26**
**Management of a
    Bed 30**

The importance of good stabling, whatever its scale, cannot be over-emphasised. First of all siting and layout are of prime concern, whether it is for a single stable or a complete range. A neat, compact layout will save unnecessary work, and ideally stables should be south-facing so that cold north or east winds do not blow in. Remember that new boxes are subject to planning permission, so when designing a stable yard allow enough space, if possible, for the erection of additional boxes that might be required in the future. Of course available funds will always influence design and layout. Other important considerations would be the accessibility of water and electricity supplies, the provision of sound drainage, and convenience of access. If correctly done, old farm buildings can be converted into excellent boxes, though this can be an expensive undertaking.

Where a number of horses are kept, an isolation box is a good idea so that in the event of a horse going down with a cough or infectious skin disease, the affected animal can be segregated from the rest of the horses.

The keeping of horses in stalls seems to be a dying practice; their use would appear to be restricted to animals that need to be housed on a day-time basis, such as for trekking or perhaps polo ponies, and occasionally a riding school.

There is an increasing trend for internal stabling, with widely varying examples ranging from one or two boxes to the fifty-horse complex. The well-run, busy stable yard usually has a wash box: a plain empty stable, or a specially constructed box with hot and cold running water, and fitted with infra-red heat lamps to help dry the horse; some are fitted with rubber

floors to prevent slipping. Note that particular care must be taken with a concrete floor because of the risk of slipping. The wash box in a smaller yard may double as a shoeing box or a clipping and grooming box.

Stables can be made of various materials, though wood is most commonly used, being easily erected and obviously cheaper to install than a brick building. Under no circumstances should tin or corrugated iron ever be used: these materials are hot in summer and cold in winter, and always offer the risk of the horse injuring itself. The basic measurements for a loose box are as follows: for ponies, 10 x 10ft (3 x 3m); for a small horse, 10 x 12ft (3 x 3.6m); and the usual average size for any larger type is 12 x 12ft (3.6 x 3.6m), with foaling boxes 16 x 16ft (4.8 x 4.8m).

At home we have five wooden boxes,

four of which measure 12 x 12ft (3.6 x 3.6m) and one 16 x 18ft (4.8 x 5.4m); they are lined with wood to the eaves and sit on a concrete base. These provide neat, easily manageable boxes which although tend to be hot in the summer, stay very warm in the winter. They will house quiet, sensible horses; it must be said, however, that young horses do seem to knock them about in the course of all the comings and goings of a busy yard. Next to the house stand another five boxes, 12 x 12ft (3.6 x 3.6m), constructed of concrete blocks with an asbestos roof, made by local tradesmen; they are white-washed and have blue doors. These are tougher and more suitable for housing young horses since they stand up well to a great deal of kicking and banging. The blocks used in this sort of construction must be hollow or 6 x 9in in order to make a secure stable for large horses.

A further block of five stables stands next to the covered yard; these are made in a similar way to the previous five except in their dimensions, being three at 12 x 12ft (3.6 x 3.6m) and two at 18 x 12ft (5.4 x 3.6m), the latter making large boxes for heavyweight show horses.

A further six boxes have been 'home-made' inside a former cow-house, making an excellent indoor complex. The conversion uses concrete blocks and wooden doors, all fitted with a metal grille above; these provide a sociable atmosphere for the horses stabled here, and an environment which is warm in the winter and cool in the summer. These boxes are easy to manage and therefore labour-saving, an important consideration in a busy yard.

# STABLE DESIGN
## BRICK-BUILT STABLES

A top-class small stable yard (below). The boxes are constructed of concrete blocks with wooden doors and timber and tiled roof, each box measuring 12 x 12ft (3.6 x 3.6m), rendered with concrete both inside and out making all surfaces smooth and thus easily painted. The tack room and day living accommodation can be seen at centre. The whole place is immaculate, right down to the neat gravel yard and orderly flower-bed – in vast contrast to the untidy, badly organised yard so often seen.

The advantages of this type of stable include a low level of maintenance, they are cool in summer and warm in winter, and generally horses are at freedom to look out one to another.

## AMERICAN-STYLE COMPLEX

In this sort of design the loose boxes are airy, and will effectively keep the horses at a constant cool temperature during the heat of the day. The upper half of the box is comprised of bars, so horses can see each other alongside as well as look out at whatever is going on round them. The disadvantages can be if horses do not agree with each other, when they may spend a considerable time trying to bite and kick at their neighbour, risking not only injury to themselves but damage to the stables. Having an adjacent exercise paddock is a great labour-saver because less time is spent walking horses to and from paddocks; although in temperate climates paddocks could readily become a mudbath.

The combined paddock and stable shelter system, illustrated here and typical in America, gives the animals more freedom and exercise than the confined loose box; this sort of layout is often used for resting and competition horses. It is a system known as 'spelling', where horses can wander about, play, roll and rest at will. The surface of the paddock is sand and would need to be raked daily and the droppings picked up; however the iron fencing dividing each horse would prevent any chewing and would be virtually maintenance free. This system is rarely used in the UK as people prefer to turn their horses out into fields and large paddocks in the company of others.

## WOODEN STABLES

A portable wooden stable block, inexpensive, practical and workmanlike, with a corrugated felt roof. It is built on a concrete pad with a central drainage channel which appears to be very poorly constructed. However, the horses can see each other, and it would be an easy yard to keep tidy. These are often portable, and the least expensive type of stable to erect. They are, however, more vulnerable to wear and tear, and need regular maintenance.

Wooden interiors are apt to be chewed, though regular creosoting will help to discourage this. Putting a metal strip over the half doors and round the surrounds, and lining the eaves of wooden boxes, also helps to prevent chewing.

The person with just one horse or pony and with limited space will find that not only is the modern wooden loose box simple to have erected by the local dealer but, coupled with a rack box where hay and straw might be stored, it does make an ideal small unit. These boxes can be painted to look even more attractive. They can cost from approximately £500 for a single box to approximately £2,000 for a complete unit. One possible disadvantage is that a young horse or pony may learn to chew the woodwork, or may kick out the odd board.

## THE LODDON CONVERSION

These boxes are often fitted into existing buildings, or can be custom-built, as shown here. This modern conversion has no grilles fitted except at the windows. The top window is open for extra ventilation. In some conversions, and sometimes in old traditional boxes, sliding doors are fitted; these are excellent providing the operator is careful to open them wide enough when allowing a horse through, and as long as the running channels are kept clean.

## INTERNAL STABLING

Internal stabling can be fitted to existing buildings or constructed as a custom-built block. The main advantage for horses kept completely indoors is that they enjoy a constant temperate atmosphere and dry surroundings, cool in summer and warm in winter, providing that adequate ventilation is installed. On the whole, grooms prefer to have their horses under one roof as each individual animal is easily accessible and the time taken to do yard duties can be cut in half.

The more traditional internal stabling block also illustrated has iron bars to the front but solid walls between, although there is a grille set into each partition wall which can be opened or left shut depending on the horse's temperament. Some people would consider this design very confining to the horse – its advantages are that horses cannot fight between themselves, or put their heads out which might encourage weaving, or biting other horses as they are led by. This block has a neat brick floor which although non-slip is probably not easy to keep clean. Moreover the yard appears to be on the dark side, and although fluorescent strip lighting is provided, this would probably need to be kept on during working hours which could be very costly.

An American internal system, of modern iron design, is easily cleaned and requires minimal maintenance; it could prove noisy, however, were horses to bang or kick. It is a successful system in areas of hot climate.

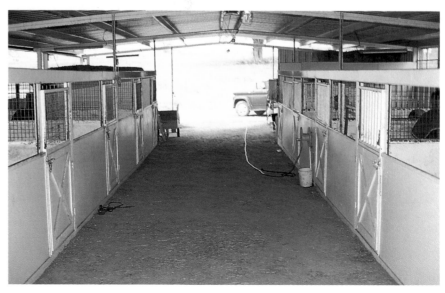

## STALLS

Horses do not generally thrive as well as they do in loose boxes, and youngsters in particular are never as happy or contented as they are in a loose box. The reasons for this may be manifold: firstly, a horse in a stall is always approached from behind, whereas it is his natural instinct to face the person approaching; when an animal is constantly tied up it must be very boring; and horses always seem reluctant to lie down in a stall. Also there is always the risk of them breaking loose and damaging themselves or other animals, although a safety chain can be put across the back of the stall to prevent this. Thus, apart from the odd yard it is not common these days to see horses in stalls – possibly there are some in army or other forces' buildings, and maybe the occasional trekking centre would have some still in use. The only advantages of a stall would seem to be that less bedding is used, and they are much quicker to muck out. Individual stalls average from 6–8ft (2–2.6m) wide, 10ft (3m) deep, and the passage behind should be no less than 6ft (2m) wide.

## FLOORING/DRAINAGE

The choice of materials used for floors is as varied as those used for the building of the stable itself, and they all have advantages and drawbacks; however, the most important points to look out for in any flooring for horses are that it should be non-slip, long-lasting, and impervious to moisture (unless it is an earth floor). Concrete is the most popular; it is reasonable in price and long-lasting, however it must be roughened on the surface to prevent it becoming dangerously slippery. Rubber matting is now more fashionable, especially for competition horses or brood mares and foals; it obviates injuries such as capped hocks, it is warmer, and less bedding is needed.

An expensive drainage system in a stable is not necessary; a gentle slope towards the outside of the box is all that is required. Drains actually in the box are unnecessary; moreover they tend to become easily blocked up with straw or shavings, they can crack, or a hoof could become trapped.

## THE BARN CONVERSION

More and more barns are being redesigned so horses can be 'yarded' inside them, particularly on farms and studs. This means that horses can be wintered under cover, but with greater freedom than is offered by a stable. As well as helping to avoid poaching of fields in wet winters and preventing complaints such as mud fever and rain scald which are associated with wet, cold and dirty conditions, it is easier to keep a closer eye on horses when yarded, and spot problems quickly. In the field it could be easy to miss any problems or complaints.

When wintering out horses they need plenty of feed, either hay, concentrates or both. They do not need so much to eat if kept inside and being under cover in bad weather helps the horse to keep its condition. They will usually look better for early shows and youngsters that are wintered in this way will not look poor for summer shows. The barns can be labour-saving in as much as they can be deep-littered, and mucked out by machine when necessary. Horses can spend part of the day out and come into the buildings at night. They are particularly useful for sick or injured animals whose exercise must be restricted.

Care should be taken to fasten down any movable objects such as hay racks. It is best to avoid cattle racks in which a horse can get itself entangled or which can be pulled down. Water holders should be fixed securely and buckets should be avoided as they become chewed, trampled upon and broken. Automatic water bowls are the best type which should be checked daily. Any centre roof supports in the barn should be encased to prevent the horse from knocking itself. Old rubber tyres prove useful for this. Any other articles such as jump wings and poles should always be removed.

## AMERICAN BARN SYSTEM

In America the barn system, where horses of the same age run together, is widely used; this means that a number of horses can be housed under one roof in deep litter, thus saving labour. However, injuries from biting and kicking can occur – though once the horses have settled they quickly establish a pecking order. This system has been tried in the UK with average results.

# VENTILATION

Ventilation is essential in all stabling: experience has shown that horses keep fitter and succumb to fewer coughs and colds when they have adequate fresh air – though it is important to avoid creating draughts which could cause chills and will make the horses' coats look rough and stary. Windows should be high, and in timber stables it is advisable to have openings at the ridges to allow stale air to escape. If stables smell stuffy the ventilation is almost certainly inadequate. In fact horses do not suffer from colds, as such, in the way that humans do; therefore top doors should always be kept open, except in severe weather. Ventilation in loose boxes will be much improved by windows which slope upwards, when the air is thrown up and over the horse.

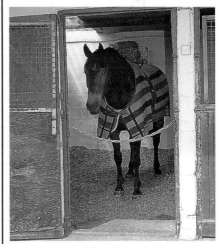

Chains across the door: horses that are quiet can look out and enjoy an uninterrupted view; also in hot weather it allows maximum circulation of fresh air. However, special care must be taken that the horse does not try and barge out; and grooms must take care when entering the stable under a chain not to startle the horse which might increase the risk of being kicked.

## VICES

Constant stabling will easily make the horse bored and often stable vices can occur. Prevention is vital as total cures are seldom found. In the first place the horse should not be imprisoned in its stable unless injury prevents movement. If grazing is limited a turn out in the field or paddock is best, even if it is only for a short spell, as this will help the horse relax which is very important. If grazing is not possible the horse could be led out in hand and allowed to pick at grass. A horse walker is ideal for exercising more than one horse at a time.

When stabled the horse should have plenty to look at as well as easy access to hay twenty-four hours a day, or, alternatively, be fed at regular intervals throughout the day.

Daily exercise will help prevent boredom, especially if work can be varied. A contented horse is less likely to pick up bad habits and vices, such as weaving, crib-biting, wood-chewing, windsucking. A collar will help to prevent windsucking, although the horse in the photo is still managing to crib-bite; a fitted grille will largely prevent this, and also weaving. A horse may also 'box walk', when he walks continually in circles, round and round his stable; rubber tyres or even a couple of bales of straw may help distract him and interrupt the habit, and the company of a sheep or a goat is often an effective preventative.

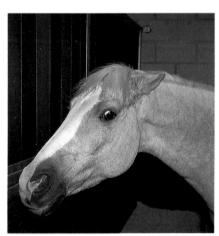

# STABLE FITMENTS

## DOORS AND GRILLES

The dimensions of the stable doorway are, ideally, 4ft (1.2m) wide and 8ft (2.4m) high; the bottom half-doors should be 4ft 6in (1.4m) high. It is essential to have doors high and wide enough to enable the free passage of a horse in and out of the stable – if a horse repeatedly hits his head or hip while entering or leaving, he will in future always tend to rush, and may become increasingly difficult to lead in and out.

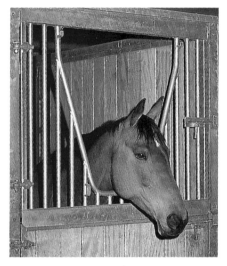

It is now common practice in many yards to have a door grille fitted, its main uses being to prevent horses weaving, biting and chewing the door frames, and to prevent youngstock from attempting to jump out. Another point to remember is that at feeding times many horses will bang the bottom door, and this can damage their

knees. It is possible to have grilles that are fitted to the bottom door, as in the first illustration; or removable; or some people prefer a 'V'-shaped grille which allows the horse to look out (as shown).

If the grille fitted to the top half of the door is too low or too small, horses will still be able to make contact; the stables illustrated would be better suited to smaller animals which would not be able to reach the top of the grilles. However, as long as neighbouring horses are compatible no harm will be done – if they are not, they will constantly fight and kick and may well cause damage to themselves and to the stables.

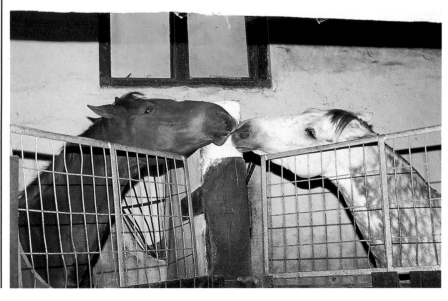

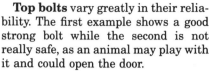

## BOLTS

It is essential that stable doors are fitted with a bottom bolt; the easiest is the **kick-over bolt**, which is both strong and easy to operate. Without a bottom bolt fitted an animal risks trapping a leg between the door and the door-post.

**Top bolts** vary greatly in their reliability. The first example shows a good strong bolt while the second is not really safe, as an animal may play with it and could open the door.

**NOTE:** It is essential that all door fittings are maintained in excellent condition, with hinges and bolts oiled regularly.

## FEEDING APPLIANCES

**Forage:** There are various ways of feeding hay to stabled horses.

Hay racks have the advantage of being less time-consuming than haynets, being easy to fill when feeding wedges of hay – though more difficult if the hay is loose or well shaken up. Hay racks vary in capacity, the smaller ones taking two to four wedges of hay, the larger racks much more. The bars of a metal hay rack must not be too close otherwise the horse will not be able to pull the hay out to eat. Hay racks are ideal for youngstock if not too high up. They should be bolted securely, at eye level.

Haynets are most commonly used to feed hay; it is easy to weigh, wet and soak hay in them, and they will also prevent wastage. Hay in nets must always be of *good quality*, as an animal cannot sort the good from the not-so-good quality hay as it would be able to in a rack or on the floor. If Horse-Hage is to be fed in nets, then the holes of the net must be small so as to prevent the horse eating it too quickly. The disadvantages of a haynet are that a horse may become entangled with its front or hind legs, particularly as empty nets hang low; they can then be hazardous. Generally a net should be hung about 6ft (2m) high for the average horse; it should be properly secured at all times, and broken nets must not be used until they are repaired.

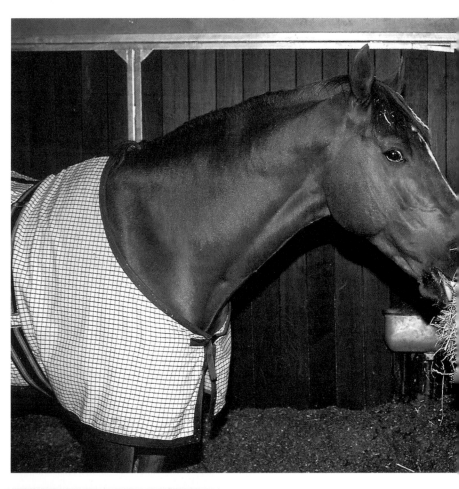

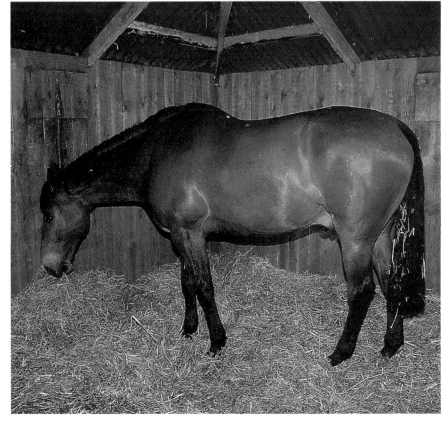

Feeding hay from the floor is probably the safest, and possibly the best way, except that some horses will waste it. This is the most natural way of feeding forage, as the horse in the wild will normally eat at floor level. If straw bedding is used this works quite well; however, with paper or shavings there may be more mess and wastage as it is more likely to become mixed up in bedding and is then difficult to manage. This system works well if a horse is on a low hay ration, for example a competition animal.

**Mangers:** The manger is an essential part of a stable's equipment, and they come in many forms. With so many to choose from, take care that the feeding manger you select does suit your individual needs. A good safe manger is a must, and will undoubtedly save time and money in wasted food and injury. The traditional version is made of cast iron and is a permanent fixture; these are fine, although not always easy to keep clean. Others include the brick or concrete corner manger; large and deep, they are used mainly in boxes made of the same materials.

Large, portable metal corner mangers can also be used and are a popular and sound investment. Horses do tend to chew wood supports, however and these must be treated regularly to discourage the habit. Plastic corner mangers are light and easy to keep clean, though horses seem to like playing with them; they are best supported by metal gains.

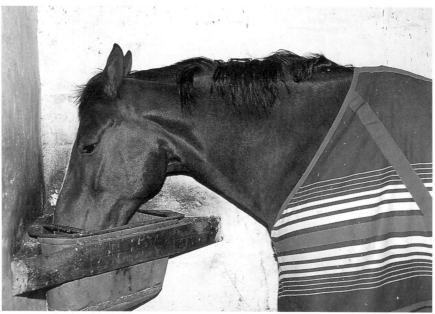

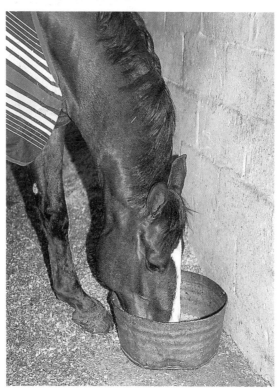

Round bins made of rubber or metal and placed on the floor may be used for youngstock. Also floor mangers can be made permanent which may be useful in some cases.

## THE DRINKING SUPPLY

Providing the stabled horse with water is of great importance to its welfare: a constant, clean supply is essential, and gone are the days when stabled horses were watered merely twice a day from an outside tank – they should have access to water at all times, except prior to a period of hard work. **Bucket watering** is still the way accepted by the majority of people. All buckets – rubber, plastic or metal – should be washed and cleaned regularly; they can be placed in a corner or in a metal bucket holder. Two buckets of water should be provided at night to prevent a horse going short. If medication in water is necessary then bucket watering is the only solution.

The **automatic waterbowl** allows the horse a constant supply of water at all times, and in hot weather and hot climates, this is essential. However, it is not possible to administer medication in waterbowls. They must be checked at least once a day to be sure they are in working order, because if they have become blocked, great distress may be caused to the horse. Equally, an overflowing waterbowl will quickly flood a shavings bed. In severe weather conditions – frosts and such-like – they may freeze over, in which case you must take care to keep them free-flowing; one helpful measure would be to lag the pipes supplying the bowls.

There are many different types of waterbowl available and all are now very reliable *if* properly maintained and installed; if these measures are taken, they provide a labour-saving and efficient way of watering. However, the waterbowl method does mean that it is difficult to tell how much a horse is drinking, which may be important if it is ill. A horse may be expected to drink six to ten gallons a day. When horses are hot and sweating it is best to offer chilled (ie warm (blood-heat)) water.

# GENERAL STANDARDS

It is important to keep the stable yard clean and tidy – the first impressions of a yard always depend upon the standards of tidiness and cleanliness, and these will inevitably reflect the standard of care devoted to the horses. Thus a visitor may assume that if a yard is clean and tidy, whatever the time of day, then the horses, too, will be enjoying a high standard of care.

Regular routine and maintenance work is vital: last thing at night the yard should be tidied in readiness for the next day. A yard should always be kept free of vermin. Any empty stables should be washed and disinfected, and painted if necessary – Snowcem wash paint is ideal for walls, and creosote for wood. Regular disinfecting of all stables will keep infectious diseases at bay.

All gravel areas should be kept weed-free and should be raked regularly, and concrete or cobbled areas swept. All gates and doors should be kept fastened at all times as swinging fixtures are dangerous.

## DRAINAGE

Good drainage in and around the yard and stables is most important; it is essential that all yard drains are cleaned regularly and all the channels kept clear. In the yard itself drains are best open-grated with a silt trap actually in the drain box.

## FIRE

Fire is undoubtedly the most horrific incident that can happen in any stable yard, particularly as horses are instinctively terrified of smoke and flames. Great care must be taken at all times to prevent any likelihood of fire. For instance, smoking should *never* be allowed in or near the stables, and in order to enforce this, signs should be prominently displayed. Fire drill with all staff should be carried out regularly, and fire extinguishers should be provided throughout the yard; these should also be serviced regularly and all staff should be familiar with their use and operation. In case of emergency, a telephone should be easily accessible, and both the police and the fire station should be called. As part of emergency equipment a fire hose may be installed, and also sand buckets may be made up, at relatively low cost.

The burning of waste materials should always be carried out well away from buildings and muck heaps. Above all, the importance of responsible behaviour in any accommodation, especially if it is over or near the stable building, should be emphasised to prevent any likelihood of fire.

In the event of fire, human life should always come before equine.

## SAFETY FIRST!

Safety in and around the stables is most important for both horses and humans alike. Untidy, dirty yards are dangerous. Forks or tools left lying about are a risk, and even a loose stone may cause lameness in the horse, or a person to trip up and perhaps even break a bone. Old horseshoes left lying about can cause injury quite easily particularly if the nails are still attached – and even the dog bowl, if it is tin, may cause a horse to shy and get loose from its handler and be injured.

Barrows are always a hazard if not stored away properly or propped up against the wall. All ladders and steps should be well maintained and carefully used. Pieces of timber, especially with old nails in, should always be piled up. The area around any repair work where workmen are still busy should be checked for stray nails old and new, as horses pick up nails in their feet quite easily. Vehicles carelessly parked are a hazard, and proper areas should be designated for parking. Lastly, to maintain standards all strings should be kept in a bag or container.

## MOUNTING BLOCKS

Mounting blocks come in all shapes and sizes. The traditional stone-built ones are the safest and the best, particularly when training a horse to be mounted from a block. Mounting from the ground on one side causes considerable stress, not only for the horse but also as wear and tear on the saddle and stirrup leather, particularly by the heavyweight rider. The use of a mounting block can often save breeches and coat from being torn; this is especially true when wearing heavyweight hunting clothes. With practice a horse will soon get used to having the rider above him for mounting, and he should always be taught to remain motionless before *and after* his rider is settled in the saddle. This is an important aspect in a horse's schooling, and a horse that has been taught to stand still for his rider at a mounting block should also do so, and thus be easier to manage, when he or she mounts from the ground.

A portable steel mounting block is not recommended; unless the horse was very quiet its sharp edges could prove very dangerous. A portable wooden block is much safer.

## STABLE TOOLS

Whether you have one horse or twenty, you will need yard tools. Buy the best tools you can as they will last the longest; if carefully maintained – wash regularly, and store by hanging on a wall – they really will last a long time. A good set will include:

1 Metal **lawn rake** for yard, gravel and muck heap
2 Good, strong, hard-bristle **yard broom**
3 **Shavings forks**; there are many different styles available, but all do the same job
4 **Four-pronged muck fork** with long or short handle
5 **Three-pronged muck fork**, often called a Newmarket fork or stable lad's fork
6 **Two-pronged hay and straw-handling fork**
7 Large, light **shovel**; the aluminium ones are very good
8 **A wheelbarrow;** this should be large enough for mucking out into and carrying hay and straw in. Several varieties are available, and some are purpose built for stable duties, made of wood or metal, both of which are excellent. Select a wheelbarrow according to price range and the number of horses stabled

**Four-wheeled trucks** are useful where a large number of horses are to be mucked out or fed hay at the same time – they will carry bales safely and without waste around the yard

**Mucking out sheets** made of plastic material are handy but are hard to carry if the handles are not strong

**Skips or skeps** for droppings can be made of metal, plastic or rubber; one common practice is to use wash-baskets (the plastic type are excellent)

9 **Hosepipe** All stable yards should have a heavy duty hosepipe for various jobs; note that cheap ones will not last as they split easily. They should be stored on a wheel to keep them out of the way

# BEDDING MATERIALS

If the horse is to survive in a stabled environment a good bed is necessary for a number of reasons. First, it will encourage the horse to lie down and rest thus minimising stress and strain on feet and legs, and also the risk of strain-type injuries. A deep, soft bed will reduce the likelihood of injuries such as capped hocks, often caused when the horse has to get up and down with insufficient bedding beneath him, and it will help to keep feet and legs warm throughout the day and night. Moreover it will allow the horse plenty of space in which to stale – horses are fussy about where they do this and are very reluctant to stale on a bare floor; regular staling is vital for the general well-being of the horse.

A bed which is light in colour is preferable as it is easier to distinguish the wet patches and to muck out. Any stabled light-coloured horses will be more readily stained by a heavily soiled dark-coloured bed.

The cost of any particular bedding material is a significant factor to consider when choosing what to use, whether for a single horse or for a large yard. The amount of bedding required each week will, however, depend on the amount of time the horse is stabled each week; the size of the stable; the size of horse; the availability of the bedding chosen and the season (if straw is used).

When obtaining a bedding material of any type it is important to inquire the size of the unit; in particular shavings can be bought in different sized bales, usually distinguished by weight. It is therefore probably worth-

while shopping around to find the best price for the heaviest bales. Straw bales are available in various sizes, though the big round bales, and the Heston bales weighing half a tonne or a tonne are difficult to manoeuvre and store. The best way to buy straw is in small bales as these are easy to manage and are least wasteful.

Similarly it is always a good idea to inquire if there is a delivery charge for the bedding; if so, it may be possible to share a delivery, and therefore costs, with a neighbour. When it arrives in your yard, always check that the straw or shavings is of the quality that you ordered, as it will be costly to send back after the lorry has left. Keep all delivery invoices in case you have a problem at a later date, or if you want to re-order.

## STRAW

(½–1 bale per day)

This is probably the most commonly used bedding type and is certainly the cheapest and usually the easiest to obtain. Three types of straw are used: wheat, barley and oat. Only wheat straw is non-palatable to the horse and this is therefore the most preferable of the three. Barley straw is palatable to the horse but it is not easily digested; it can therefore be a cause of colic as it may ball up in the horse's digestive tract and cause impaction. Similarly oat straw is palatable and may cause digestive upsets. Further, both barley and oat straw may provoke eye problems as the orms of the shafts of the straw can easily get into the horse's eye.

### ADVANTAGES

1 Easy to dispose of: it may be used by contractors as mushroom compost, or can be burnt in a safe place
2 Easy to obtain and store
3 Cheap and economical to use
4 Managed as a drainage bed, any wetness drains away from the surface and is therefore not in contact with the horse's skin when it lies down. The illustration shows a brick stable with the straw put to the sides and floor swept clean, to allow it to dry while the horse is out of its box
5 It stays fresh and hygienic for a long time if managed correctly

### DISADVANTAGES

1 It may cause digestive problems if eaten (oat and barley straw)
2 Dusty straw may cause coughs
3 Wheat straw has long stalks and may be difficult to manage
4 Some horses show an allergic reaction to the dust in straw
5 Fungi may grow in the straw banks edging the bed if these are not properly managed, and the spores may cause lung problems

## SHAVINGS

(3 bales per week)

Although expensive, this bedding is extremely effective and hygienic. It is absorbent, and is ideal in stables where the floor is not free-draining.

### ADVANTAGES

1 Clean and hygienic
2 Very good for horses that cough or show an allergic reaction when bedded on straw
3 Shavings are excellent to manage either as a deep-litter bed or a bed that is mucked out every day
4 This type of bedding can be stored outside as it is delivered in plastic bags

### DISADVANTAGES

1 Difficult to dispose of as it is slow to rot and cannot be spread on the land as can straw waste
2 Foreign bodies such as nails or sharp pieces of wood are sometimes present in poor quality shavings
3 It is costly to start and maintain a shavings bed
4 Bales are heavy to handle; it is heavy to work when wet
5 This type of bedding may dry the feet if the horse is stabled all the time

## PAPER

(3 bales per week)

This type of bedding is similar to shavings in both nature and management. It is becoming increasingly popular, particularly in racing and eventing yards where it is important that horses are prevented from eating their bedding. It is also ideal for horses which suffer from any sort of wind problem, as it eliminates all types of dust. Paper is shredded and bought packed in bales; it is usually two-thirds the price of shavings. On the other hand, a deep bed is required as paper is not as absorbent as straw or shavings; and its main disadvantage is that it tends to blow off from the muck heap. Most suppliers of horse products will also supply paper bales.

### ADVANTAGES

1 Light and easy to handle
2 Good for horses with respiratory problems such as COPD
3 Very warm
4 Easy to muck out as it is light in colour and weight

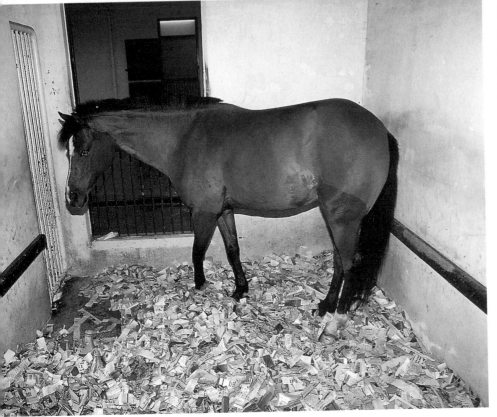

**5** Prevents horses eating their bedding, so the amount a horse eats daily can be carefully monitored (for example competition horses)

DISADVANTAGES
**1** Difficult to dispose of: it cannot be used in agriculture for soil improvement, and disposal by fire might be dangerous as large lumps of burning paper waste may be carried on the wind
**2** Paper may be difficult to obtain as it is a specialist by-product
**3** If not properly managed fungal growth may occur, causing lung problems

## PEAT MOSS

3–4 bales for 10 x 12ft (3 x 3.6m) box

This type of bedding is commonly used in Ireland, the Pennines and Scotland where it is readily available. There it is practical and economical to use.

Peat moss as bedding is particularly valuable where the risk of fire is a consideration. Wet, soiled patches must be taken out and the bed forked over frequently to prevent it becoming packed and soggy. Peat moss is normally supplied packed down in plastic bales, in the same way as wood shavings. The number of bales needed for a new bed depends on the size of the stable, and the depth of bed required.

ADVANTAGES
**1** No respiratory problems apparent
**2** Warm and absorbent
**3** Easy disposal

DISADVANTAGES
**1** Not very pleasing to the eye
**2** Very heavy and hard to manage
**3** Difficult to store
**4** As it is dark in colour it can be difficult to locate the wet areas

## AUBIOSE (illustrated right)

3–4 bales for 12 x 12ft (3.6 x 3.6m) box

Aubiose has even more to recommend it than either shavings or paper. It is derived from the soft centre of the hemp plant, a fast-growing annual used principally for the manufacture of fine paper, and grown entirely without the use of any sort of chemical pesticide

or fertiliser. The raw material is graded into particles about half the size of wood shaving but much softer, and in character it is like a natural sponge – it can absorb up to twelve times more water than straw and four times more than shavings. It is very warm and also highly durable, and because of all these factors is easy to manage. It is thoroughly dust-extracted before being packed into plastic bags. Because it is produced from young plants, Aubiose breaks down rapidly into humus after use, and as an unadulterated natural product, is highly acceptable to any organically run garden, nursery or farm.

ADVANTAGES
**1** Light to handle
**2** Excellent for horses that suffer any sort of respiratory problems, or are allergic to dust
**3** Warm, and highly absorbent so the bed remains dry
**4** Lasts longer, and requires less maintenance, than other fibre bedding materials
**5** It is a highly fertile organic fertiliser, and is therefore easy to dispose of

DISADVANTAGES
**1** Initial set-up cost slightly higher

## RUBBER MATTING

Approx initial cost £200–£400 per box

Rubber is sometimes used as an alternative bedding material but it is very much in the experimental stages. Although very expensive to buy and install, it usually proves to be an excellent long-term investment: bedding material of any other kind must be replaced constantly, whereas rubber matting has a life expectancy of around 10 years. This type of bedding can be used on its own or with the minimum of extra bedding.

ADVANTAGES
**1** Long-lasting

DISADVANTAGES
**1** Not very pleasing to the eye
**2** Cold in winter
**3** A horse lying in its own droppings will always be dirty
**4** Does little to prevent a horse getting cast

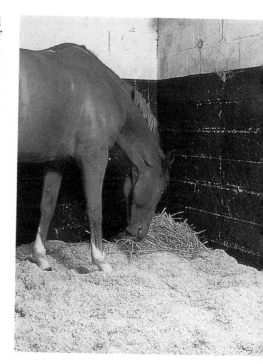
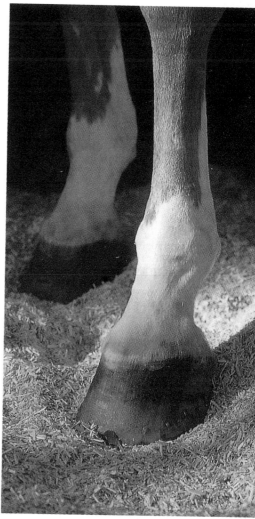

# MANAGEMENT OF A BED

Before laying down any bedding it is important that the floor is clean and dry, and that the box has been checked. The walls should be scrubbed clean, and wood should be treated with creosote and brick white-washed. With extra large stables it is not necessary or economical to bed the whole area, perhaps just half or three-quarters; this may be done according to where the fixtures of the box are positioned.

The average box of 12 x 12ft (3.6 x 3.6m) will take 3–4 bales of straw (small size), or 4–5 bales of shavings. The size and weight of the horse to be stabled will dictate how much bedding is laid down – for example a heavy horse will quickly compact a new bed and make it thin; so it is always better to provide a little too much bedding when starting off a bed, to compensate for the amount it will settle. Whatever the bedding material, it is important to bank it high round the sides of the bed and box in order to reduce the risk of the horse becoming cast when lying down or rolling and incurring injury.

There are various methods of managing a bed of any type: it may be deep litter, or mucked out every day, or it may be a combination of these two systems called a semi-deep-litter bed (illustrated) when it is cleaned out thoroughly each week or fortnight. Whatever you decide, remember that constant careful management of any type of bed will help to keep rugs and blankets in good order, and the horses themselves cleaner.

## DEEP-LITTER BEDS

The larger stable will be easier to manage and is obviously better suited to a deep-litter system; in particular youngstock that are turned out by day are more easily managed on deep litter as the bed can be put straight, and it has a chance to dry out while they are out. Moreover in the cold and wet of winter the deep-litter bed will be warmer and more practical. Depending on the individual animal and the type of bedding and stabling used, it may last six months. However, extra preparation of the stable will be required before the bed is started as any woodwork will deteriorate more quickly if bedding is not moved every day; in particular this applies to portable boxes which are lined with a non-durable wood such as plyboard. This

type of box may be lined with plastic sheeting or given an extra coat of creosote.

Any deep-litter bed is started in the same way as a 'normal' bed – only the management will differ. Droppings should always be removed, throughout the day, last thing at night and first thing in the morning to keep the bed clean and dry, and also any waste hay to prevent it becoming mixed with the bedding making the latter wet and heavy. Once a bed has been allowed to deteriorate it will be necessary to remove the centre completely, even to take all the bedding right out and start

again. The deep-litter shavings bed illustrated has been allowed to become dirty and too deep. Note that deep-litter bedding tends to 'ball' in the hooves making them smelly and difficult to clean out, so it is important to pick them out at least twice a day.

Deep-litter straw must be managed even more assiduously than shavings as straw forms a drainage bed which will quickly deteriorate into a wet, dirty, smelly mess if not managed conscientiously; for example, droppings should be removed at least twice a day, and wet surface straw. Start the bed with at least four bales of straw, then add enough straw daily to keep the bed dry. In cold weather deep-litter straw beds are ideal as they provide warmth and encourage the horse to lie down. Peat and paper deep-litter beds need the most conscientious management of all as they very readily become wet and soggy, with disastrous consequences to a horse's feet and wind.

In hot eastern climates the ground surface is sand and this comprises the most abundant and cheap bedding; stables are built straight on the sand where the wet will drain away and the droppings may be easily removed. Fresh sand is brought into the stable as we would supply fresh bedding. However, sand is a mineral and some horses will eat it, so to alleviate the problem of sand colic a mineral lick is always provided in the stable.

In the USA it is very unusual to use a deep-litter system because of the extremes of temperature; in hot climates deep litter is unusual due to the smell being very unpleasant to work with. In Australia shavings or straw are commonly used as in the UK, but not often as deep litter as many more horses are re-housed out of doors in a rotational paddock system, with stables or field shelters.

## DAILY CLEANING OUT

A stable which is to be mucked out every day requires careful and meticulous management in order for the bed to remain clean and viable. The following instructions are an easy-to-follow guide to mucking out the straw bed.

1 Assemble all tools to be used outside the box.

2 Tie up the horse, or move it to a safe place.

3 Remove the water buckets from the stable in order to prevent any muck falling into them and contaminating them (behind the stable door on the outside of the stable will be a good place).

4 Skip out the box removing all obvious droppings or wet patches. This should be done at least three times a day or whenever attention is paid to the horse; regular skipping out of all stabled horses assists in their general standard of cleanliness and well-being. Take care always to fork away from the horse; move him around the stable to your convenience.

5 Separate all the clean straw from the staled, and gradually work over the whole bed until the floor is clear.

6 Turn over a bank a day; once the floor has been swept and if possible allowed to dry, bring the straw from that bank to make the centre of the new bed.

7 The new bedding that will be brought to freshen the bed may now be used to make the third bank.

If possible it is a good idea to leave the bed to settle for a few minutes; this minimises the dust in the air before the horse is brought back and the water buckets replaced.

Using this simple system the whole bed will be turned over every three days and will therefore remain clean and fresh all the time. If the horse is to be turned out or is to be away for the day it is always a good idea to leave the bed up for the day so the floor can dry out thoroughly.

## MUCK MANAGEMENT

A tidy muck heap is a must, and an untidy one will be glaringly obvious in an otherwise tidy yard. Thus muck heaps should be kept square and well trodden around the edges, and stacked tidily each day. The site should be chosen with care, taking into consideration the following factors: drainage; prevailing wind; access (it should be central to the yard and convenient both for mucking out and removal); it should not be too close to buildings as it may be a fire risk; it is best sited on a hard surface to prevent poaching round about.

Shavings and paper waste are more difficult to dispose of than straw as they are of no use to mushroom contractors or farmers unless they have been rotted down over a long period of time. These bedding types cannot be spread easily on the land.

If the muck heap is to be burnt, it must be done at certain times of the day by law, as neighbours and horses alike object to smoke and flames.

Stable barrows made of metal, wood or plastic are also available. The horse should always be tied up to prevent the risk of him charging the door and getting entangled in the barrow, especially a young animal. Never use a barrow inside the box when there is a horse inside.

The whole yard can be mucked out straight into this trailer (left), to save time and sweeping; it is very convenient for deep litter or semi-deep litter. It is also used for carrying bedding to the various stables, and assists in numerous other jobs in the stable yard.

## SAFETY POINTS

NEVER

1 Leave tools in the stable
2 Leave the horse untied when working in the box
3 Bring a wheelbarrow right into the stable or leave it unattended in a doorway: the inquisitive nature of horses puts them at risk of injury through getting entangled with stable equipment
4 Leave water buckets and mangers in the stable

ALWAYS

1 Fork away from the animal
2 Tidy away as you work
3 Note any unusual things as you work – for example if the bed seems unusually disturbed in the morning it may denote that the horse has suffered a bout of colic in the night, or has been cast
4 Check for foreign bodies – sticking out nails and suchlike – that may cause damage to the horse

# 2
# FIELDS AND FENCING

Fencing  40
Gates  45
Field Shelters  46
The Water Supply  49
Feeding in the
    Field  50
Pasture
    Maintenance  51

When horses and ponies are kept outdoors, whether in summer or winter, or for all or part of the time, it is of the utmost importance that they are provided with a safe and suitable environment, and checked once, preferably twice, each day. Horses thrive best of all on a limestone soil; limestone is, of course, mainly calcium, and contains all the various elements that are required for optimum growth and development and in particular for bone growth. This is why Ireland is such a famous breeding ground.

In modern farming, land can be improved greatly by means of liming, as this will boost the calcium content and help combat weed encroachment, since weeds will not thrive in an alkaline soil. However, good drainage coupled with clean, fertile land will inevitably provide an environment in which horses will thrive. Furthermore, most drainage problems can be overcome by means of deep ploughing or sub-soiling (when a hook is 'dragged' through the soil to make a drainage channel).

Nowadays when pasture is first laid down it is possible to have either a grass seed mix formulated to your own needs, or to buy a ready-mixed pasture seed especially for horses. During the winter in a wet, temperate climate such as prevails in the UK, horses tend to tread and poach grassland to an unacceptable degree, particularly if they run out the whole time; if possible they are better restricted to a limited acreage and fed extra feed, rather than being allowed to gallop around cutting up large areas. The rested land will then be more 'forward' in spring.

Take care that in winter-time, horses do not lose condition, particularly if they are fed out of doors; this task should be carried out with adequate forethought. For example, hay can be fed either in a rack, in haynets or loose on the ground, though the latter can be very wasteful unless carefully watched. A concentrate feed given outdoors should never be placed on the ground as this is extremely wasteful; besides, there are many and various outdoor containers that can be purchased for outdoor feeding – one of the best for youngstock is the round container which fits into a vehicle tyre.

When the spring grass starts to appear horses will often benefit if they continue to receive a concentrate feed, but with less hay, in order to maintain condition; at this time of year they will often 'go off' hay and lose condition, especially when they are changing their coats. It is essential to move the position of feeding places to avoid undue poaching of the ground – and *never* feed in or around the gateways where easy access is required.

During the summer months a horse or pony at rest or in light work only should not require additional feeding, except perhaps Thoroughbred horses. In fact in spring and summer there is nearly always a flush of grass, and some horses and ponies may need to be restricted in their grazing areas to prevent them becoming grossly fat and possibly incurring certain health disorders; some of them will even need to be brought into the stable or yard and 'starved' for part of the day or the night.

# FENCING

The best type of fencing for horses is wooden post and rail, particularly if backed by a thick, non-palatable hedge or belt of trees to provide shelter from wind and rain. Any form of wire fence carries a much higher risk of injury should horses become entangled in it. The following series of photos illustrates some good, and some not so good, methods of fencing a field or paddock for horses.

The ultimate in safe, effective and attractive fencing for horses (right): if properly maintained, this **post-and-rail** fencing is the best that money can buy. Although at £5–£10 a yard it is costly, it will last a lifetime and is therefore economic on a long-term basis. This fence is about 4ft 6in (1.4m) high with rails at intervals: note that the rails are on the inside of the uprights; also the high hazel and beech hedge which will serve as an excellent wind-break – nor will horses eat it.

A new stained **post-and-rail** fence backed by a recently planted thuja hedge: these trees make an excellent quick-growing wind-break, especially if they are planted during autumn or winter when they become established easily. The more expensive beech hedge or the less expensive quickthorn make equally good shelters. This type of fence is ideal for dividing fields into paddocks.

**Railing** is the best type of fencing, but if it is not carefully maintained it soon becomes damaged; a regular dressing of creosote will prolong its life and help protect against horses chewing at the wood. The now more popular idea of running an electric wire along the top rail will help considerably, as horses leaning, straining and rubbing against the rails will loosen the upright post. These need be no wider than 15 to 20 yards (14 to 18m) apart, of planed square timber post and rail; in high class studs the fence is often painted white, though this is a luxury few of us can afford.

Crib-biting, the results of which can be seen on this fence, is not only a vice recognised in the veterinary purchase procedure, it is altogether a dangerous habit as splinters that are swallowed may cause internal disorder.

A very strong sound **post-and-rail** fence (left) with posts close together and rails securely fixed and creosoted for longer life; note that the bottom rail should never be lower than 18in (45cm) from the ground, to prevent injury.

A **badly maintained** fence, with a rail broken and now a hazard to animals that may be turned out in this field; the broken piece of fence has been left on the ground and a rusty nail may be seen sticking out of one of the uprights. Clearly the message here is that good maintenance is of the utmost importance.

A fine example of a really **stock-proof hedge with post and rail and pig-netting wire** (above); this means, of course, that the field can also be grazed by cattle and sheep as well as horses. Its only disadvantage is that there is always the danger of a horse or pony becoming entangled in the wire, either from pawing at the fence or possibly kicking back when newly turned out. This would be particularly true with youngstock.

A very sound **stock-proof** fence but not suitable for horses, and particularly risky if horses are turned out on either side of it. The main worry concerning this fence is that horses may well gallop through it, though it could be made safer by adding electric fencing to it – once horses have appreciated its exact position it may prove safe. However, this method of fencing is not to be recommended for horses.

This is the same fence as in the foregoing photograph but with a **guard-rail** added; in fact its disadvantages are the same, since there is still the danger of a horse getting a leg hung up in the wire.

A very sound, safe type of fencing which has the added protection of an electric wire unit to prevent horses chewing the rails. This is on a stud in Australia. The Australians use a lot of **electric fencing** together with their post and railing, not only to prevent horses chewing but to stop them biting each other over the fences.

Another example of Australian fencing, again **electrified**, which invariably keeps horses clear of the fence – otherwise it would be dangerous, were horses to become entangled. Once a horse has touched a live electric fence it will be very reluctant to do so again, so this type of fencing, although not ideal, will prove most effective. Its major disadvantage is that a startled or galloping horse may well not see it and could run straight through it, causing untold injury. An inexpensive yet effective way of marking a fence such as this is to cut up coloured plastic bags into strips and tie these firmly around the wire to make it easily visible to the horse. (This operation *must* be carried out while the fence is turned off.)

A combination of **tape and electrified wire**, a method used to divide up fields; this fence is particularly loose and animals would be at grave risk of becoming entangled in it. Horses need to be introduced to this type of fencing very carefully if they are not to risk injury; for example, if several were freshly turned out together they might gallop through it, not only endangering themselves, but entailing a great deal of work and unnecessary expense in sorting out the ensuing muddle and mess. If put up properly, this type of fencing may be used as a temporary method for turned out horses as it is quick and easy to erect.

**White tape** fencing is becoming more and more popular, particularly as it can be erected for both temporary or permanent use depending on the posts that are used. It is essential that it is well put up and tight – its one disadvantage after a time is that it does become slack and very soggy. It is usually made of plastic and can be purchased in various widths, though nylon is available, sometimes with a thin nylon wire running through it; generally the top piece is electrified.

**High tensile wire** fencing is used a great deal in Australia and the USA, very often to divide up large areas or paddocks. It is relatively inexpensive, and avoids the problem of horses chewing or destroying a post-and-rail construction. Usually this type of fencing is electrified, thus keeping animals away from it, and guarding against the risk of their becoming entangled in it. However, daily inspection is necessary to make sure that it has not become slack or damaged, for one reason or another.

# GATES

It is most important that gates which are used for horses are well hung so that they open and close easily. If horses are jostling around a gateway and the gate is awkward to open and gets stuck, it would be all too easy for one to try and push through the gap when it is still too narrow, perhaps causing injury to itself or its handler.

The well-maintained, well-hung gate (right) has a cross-bar for added strength.

A gate such as the one illustrated would be ideal for use in a double gate system, when a small enclosure is created within the field to help in catching difficult horses, or when attending to field-kept horses, for example when picking out their feet and so on. This double gate system may also be used if a field or paddock opens onto a main road – by having another gate as a 'safety net', accidents may be prevented. Ideally, gates used anywhere in fields should be not less than 6ft (1.8m) wide, except for hunting gates which may, in some circumstances, be used between paddocks.

## GATE FASTENINGS

It is not a good idea to have gate hooks and fasteners that protrude to any great extent, as these may easily catch

against an animal as it goes in or out and cut or hurt it. Gates should always be well hung, and all catches maintained. Never use rope or string which can be easily chewed through, consequently allowing the animals to escape. In view of the proliferation of recent thefts involving horses and horse-related property, all gates should be securely locked – remember that a gate can be lifted off its hinges, so this end should be fastened as well. Also, never leave headcollars in a field at night as this might well help a would-be thief in his efforts to catch a horse.

## MAINTENANCE

Broken down, worn-out gates should always be replaced because of their potential to cause injury. As well as the obvious cuts and tears that can be caused, there may be other less apparent damage: for example, superficial scratches may harbour the tetanus bacterium, which if contracted can prove fatal if vaccinations are not up to date. Collapsed, rusty gates must be fenced off safely, or better still removed and replaced with a gate such as the one above.

# FIELD SHELTERS

A field shelter is often seen nowadays both in this country and abroad, and is generally of huge benefit for the field-kept horse. A design with a bottom door means that the horse or pony may be shut in if the weather is bad, or fed inside separately from any others – in short, the shelter may be used as a normal stable. Another significant advantage is that horses annoyed by flies and prone to 'sweet-itch' may take refuge in it at the critical times of day.

In the event of disease, a shelter such as this may well be used as an isolation stable, where an infected horse or one with a suspected infection may be kept away from the rest of the yard.

There are certain features which should always be looked for in a well-designed shelter such as the one illustrated: it is best situated with its back to the prevailing wind; it should have an adequately high roof and wide entrance to minimise the risk of cuts and knocks if horses are jostling and bullying each other; interior fixtures – mangers, racks – must be safe and durable, and set at a sensible height; and finally, the area surrounding a shelter, and particularly the approach, should offer a firm footing.

The field shelter (right) is typical in Australia where horses are kept out much more than in temperate countries such as the UK, as the climate is generally more favourable to this type of management. The shelter that is shown is not ideal, for several reasons: firstly, it is not really high enough for larger horses which would risk knocking themselves; secondly, although it is very durable, this type of corrugated iron may develop sharp edges as it wears. Lastly, a hard approach, maybe concrete, would be advantageous – it can be clearly seen that the grass around the shelter has been completely worn away.

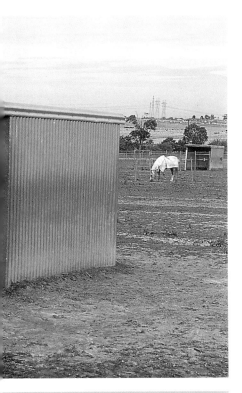

A field shelter commonly used in Australia, with many good features: the dimensions are excellent – high roof and wide entrance – and the surround offers a firm, solid footing. The framework is of treated wood, for added strength and durability; and the fixtures are at a safe height, of a plastic material that is durable and safe.

This typical Australian shelter and paddock system would probably only cost a few hundred pounds, but both shed and rails are strong and well constructed; this form of shelter would provide quite adequate protection from flies and heat, and of course tropical storms. Horses in Australia are often ridden and trained from a shelter-and-paddock environment, as they are in the USA.

A good field shelter design, although it is a little low for the ideal. It has its back to the prevailing wind which will keep it cleaner and drier, and the slatted design will maintain a good circulation of air. Its wide, open front is an excellent feature, minimising the likelihood of jealous horses jostling in the entrance way with the attendant risk of injury.

An American shelter and paddock, very expensive and used in a hot climate night and day, generally for valuable Thoroughbred stock. Horses kept like this are managed in a way similar to stabled horses in that they are also exercised and groomed daily, and the paddocks skipped out regularly. Yearlings being prepared for sales are often housed in this way.

A well-made, practical shelter and outside yard, ideal for youngstock and resting older horses. Sometimes a semi-deep-litter straw bed is laid, which in winter-time can be properly deep-littered; this means that several young animals can be kept together with minimum labour. It has an excellent outside hay rack and feed trough combined, a design which is both safe and strong.

The steel pen illustrated is used for limited exercising and for lungeing, and is especially useful when it is necessary to restrict horses that are sick or injured; it also offers a safe turn-out area for young foals and their mothers. The other design available has higher wire-mesh sides and can be used for the same variety of purpose. Both types of pen can, of course, be moved regularly to a different, fresh grazing area.

# THE WATER SUPPLY

The water supply to a field or paddock is of equal priority. A horse drinks between 8 and 15 gallons (36 to 68 litres) daily, according to its size, so it is essential to have fresh water readily available. Always check water daily to make sure the supply is still running and not blocked, or frozen solid in winter-time. Water supplied in buckets is most unreliable because this sort of container is so easily knocked over; and old baths cause injury, they are a nuisance to fill and the water risks becoming stale.

Troughs such as the one illustrated should be safe and placed so that the horses can drink without being trapped in a corner; if a water trough has not been in recent regular use it should be scrubbed and cleaned thoroughly before re-use. It is very important to bale out this type of trough, containing static water, once a week; and in winter make sure that it doesn't freeze up and so deprive the horse of water.

Ideally there should be a hard approach so the ground around the tank does not become poached and ruined as has happened here.

The best type of trough is an automatically self-filling one; these ensure that horses always have water.

A free-running stream with firm, low banks and easy access provides an ideal water source.

The stream illustrated would prove unsuitable for horses to drink from as their only source of water, mainly because the approach is bad – if they had to climb down to the water level all the time, the banks of the stream would almost certainly collapse, thus blocking the flow of water. Moreover, a stream such as this is probably not always free-flowing, for example in summer-time when the water level will drop and the water almost certainly become semi-stagnant and undesirable.

## FEEDING IN THE FIELD

Ideally horses should be brought in every day to be fed (it also provides you with an opportunity to check for injury); however, in a working situation this is rarely possible. If horses are given their hard feed in the field, it is important that their bowls are placed well away one from the other, to ensure that the right horse gets the right feed, particularly as there is bound to be an increased risk of kicking and injury if they attempt to fight over feeds. It would be best at least to put them in separate areas to be fed.

The photograph shows a badly positioned feed container; this situation could be hazardous if the horse were to become entangled in the wire fence whilst feeding.

### MINERAL AND FEED BLOCKS

For horses and ponies that are kept outside, and particularly for youngstock, mineral blocks are essential;

ideally they should be placed in a container rather than straight on the ground. Feed blocks are also now widely available; these can be fed in the autumn to supplement the declining quality of the grass. Some of these blocks have a hole in the centre so they

can be hung on a fence or tree. It is almost impossible to monitor the intake of any one horse if running out in a group, but even if it eats a lot more than the other, it is unlikely to suffer any adverse effect as horse blocks are specifically and carefully formulated.

## PASTURE MAINTENANCE

The quality of grass and variety of herbage will quite quickly fall away, and the pasture soon become sour and 'horse-sick' if paddocks are used continually and without care and attention – droppings will be seen over a large area, with very little grass and animals rather desultorily picking up pieces of hay from amongst the mud, weeds and dirt.

The paddock illustrated is typical of one that has obviously had too many animals grazing it, so it has become poached, bare and almost certainly worm-infested. To maintain a healthier pasture and a measure of controlling the worm burden, it helps in any paddock to pick up droppings as regularly as possible. Partial reseeding, rolling and rest will help restore a pasture and anyway small paddocks are best kept clear of horses if possible during the wet winter months. Grazing sheep together with horses will help tidy up uneaten areas of grass and also reduce worm infestation; and in larger fields cattle will help, though in small

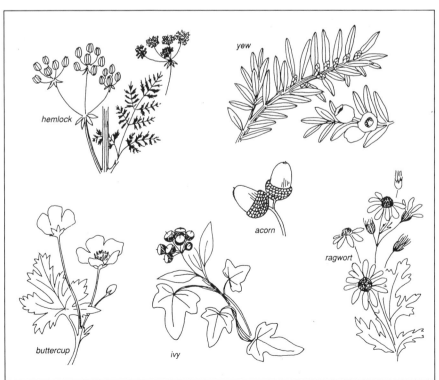

paddocks they will rub against and easily break even the best post and railing if it is not guarded by electric fencing.

Obviously holes and ruts, and very uneven footing in a field can be disastrous – if a horse puts a foot into a hole whilst galloping it could easily break a leg. Check pasture land regularly (right) to avoid these hazards. Particular care must be taken where rabbits are seen as they do burrow well away from the hedgerows and cause considerable damage: harrowing and rolling the surfaces damaged in the winter should level off the ground satisfactorily, although larger holes would have to be filled in by hand. Exercising horses over farmland and around fields in winter-time can cause considerable damage, and this will need to be carefully put right in the spring – otherwise when the ground dries out it will remain extremely poached and rutty and be virtually unridable. Topping pasture with a topping machine will level off any uneaten patches of grass and will keep the land looking tidy, and also encourage a wider eating area.

# 3
# TACK AND CLOTHING

Bits and Bridles  57
Headcollars, Halters
    and Lead-ropes  63
Saddles  64
Girths  66
Boots and
    Bandages  67
Horse Clothing  70

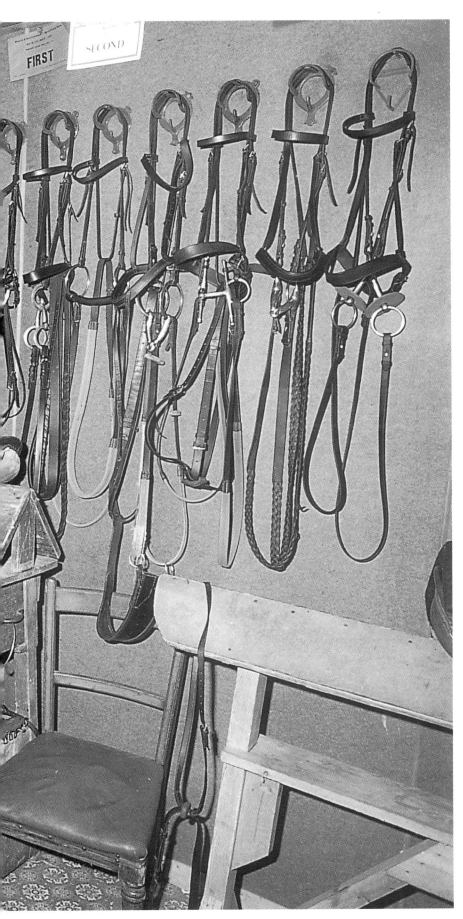

A wide variety of all types of tack and horse clothing can be seen on the market today and it is a well-known fact that to equip a horse and rider fully may easily cost more than the horse itself. Whatever you buy, care of clothing and tack is of great importance, not only in its everyday cleaning, but in storing it and, above all, in fitting and maintaining it correctly. Many a serious accident has occurred because of broken stitching or a cracked piece of leather which has gone unnoticed, and this may be prevented by proper care and observation.

The cost of a serviceable secondhand saddle may be a hundred pounds or more, and a new one may be anything up to £1,500 or even more in some special cases – though remember, *new* is not always best as regards fitting correctly, and it is sometimes as well to buy a good, well-fitting secondhand saddle than a poorly fitting, less well made, new saddle. How much you spend on tack and clothing is, of course, a matter of personal preference; but it is as well to remember that a few carefully chosen, good quality pieces of equipment or clothing means you will probably avoid having to re-buy, or have repaired frequently, poor quality goods; and by considering very carefully what is bought in the first place, you will avoid unnecessary expense. Once the horse clothing that is required has been decided upon, you will have to consider which is likely to provide the best fit for the horse: correctly fitted horse clothing is of great importance to the comfort and well-being of a horse as it is less likely to rub or slip.

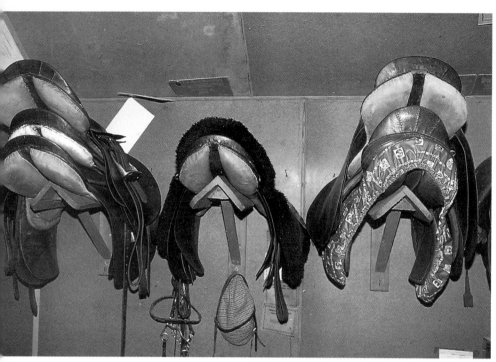

## STORING TACK

Saddles should be stored low enough to reach safely, but out of damp draughts and out of the easy reach of mice and suchlike. They can be placed on racks, either individual or a saddle horse, which can be wooden or iron, though iron ones do not always spread the weight of the saddle evenly and may disrupt the balance of the stuffing; and if not properly covered with plastic or cloth, they may scratch the leather. To be correct, they should not be put one on top of another (as can be seen in the photograph) because this practice risks stretching the trees or marking the underneath saddle.

A numnah is best put on top of a saddle after use (see the black sheep-skin numnah on top of the centre saddle): this will allow it to air, and will also go some way towards protecting the saddle from damage. Numnahs should always be kept washed and clean – failure to do so may cause a sore, rubbed back, or if shared or bought secondhand may easily spread disease.

The bridles are hung at eye level which is quite a practical way of storing them as they may be reached easily, without having to use a step. Here the groom is checking stitching and general wear and tear in the course of everyday cleaning

## CLEANING TACK

The cleaning of all tack and horse clothing is of vital importance if it is to stay safe and serviceable at all times. On a daily basis a quick wipe over with a damp cloth should be sufficient and a little saddle soap applied, but saddles and bridles should be stripped down for an extra special clean at least once a week. For a full tack clean it is necessary to have a bucket of clean warm water and sponge the leather thoroughly, removing any trace of dirt or grease. Sometimes stubborn little balls of grease appear on the saddle flaps; these are called jockeys and should not be removed by using a knife or a fingernail which will damage the leatherwork, but with a small ball of rolled-up horse hair. When dry, apply a liberal amount of saddle soap. *Never* be tempted to use boot polish as it will stain the leather and rub off on all other types of horse clothing. All metalwork should be cleaned with a metal cleaner, and must be *well* polished off after.

# BITS AND BRIDLES

There are three types of bit, the snaffle, the double bridle bits and the pelham, though there are several varieties in each category, particularly snaffles. For showing, novice horses and ponies can be ridden in a snaffle bridle and plain noseband; for open classes a double bridle should be worn, though sometimes a pelham is acceptable. There is also a showing bit which has just one mouthpiece, but the sides are constructed to make it look like a double bridle; this is particularly useful for an animal which has too small a mouth, or is upset by the two bits of a double bridle.

## THE SNAFFLE

The jointed snaffle acts on the outside of the bars of the mouth, the lips, or the corners of the mouth, according to the hand action of the rider; in conjunction with the rider's legs, it basically teaches the horse to accept the bit with a still and correct headcarriage and supple jaw. As regards fitting, it should be high enough in the mouth to cause two or three small wrinkles in the corners of the lips, and with enough room here to insert a finger on each side. The thicker the mouthpiece, the milder the effect of the bit. The following are variations on a snaffle:

1 The loose-ring jointed snaffle
2 D-ring jointed snaffle (plain metal or vulcanite)

3 Plain eggbut jointed snaffle
4 Eggbut jointed snaffle with cheekpieces – good for young horses because the cheekpiece stops the bit sliding through the mouth should stronger rein contact be needed in turning
5 Straight-bar rubber loose-ring snaffle; again, good for young horses, or those with very soft or damaged mouths

A much sharper effect will be had from the following:
1 Eggbut snaffle with French link (double-jointed snaffle)
2 Jointed snaffle with slight twist
3 Cheek jointed snaffle with a soft twist
4 Copper roller snaffle

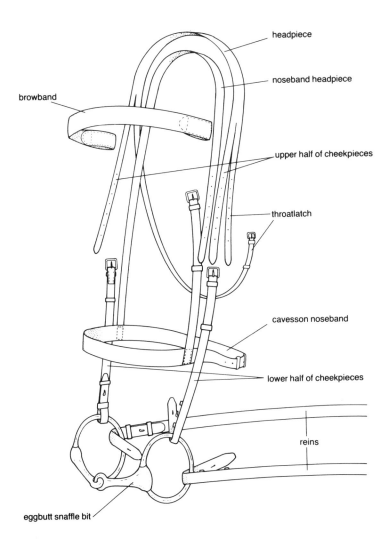

- headpiece
- noseband headpiece
- browband
- upper half of cheekpieces
- throatlatch
- cavesson noseband
- lower half of cheekpieces
- reins
- eggbutt snaffle bit

**Parts of a snaffle bridle**, showing an eggbutt snaffle

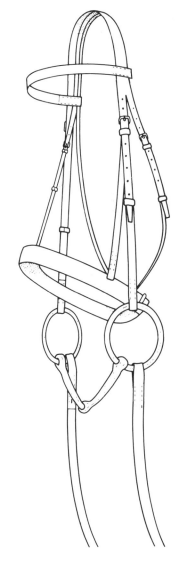

**Snaffle bridle** with loose-ring snaffle bit fitted

A snaffle bridle with *Wilson* bit, and a grakle noseband; in fact the fine leather is not very suitable for a horse with such a large head. The Wilson bit is a stronger version of the loose-ring bit. The reins are attached to the outer rings and the cheek pieces fixed on to the inner ring. The Wilson bridoon proves to be a useful bit for horses who lean or tend to become strong in the hand.

## THE DOUBLE BRIDLE

The double bridle should only be used when the horse has accepted the snaffle bridle and is generally working with confidence and contentment. It consists of a bridoon, which can be a loose-ring or egg-butt snaffle but thinner than the ones described above, and a curb bit. Variations of the curb bit are with a fixed or sliding mouthpiece and a variety of ports or tongue grooves. Experiment with different types of these bits until you find the ideal one for each horse.

The double bridle is the most commonly used bridle for the show ring and is traditionally used in the hunting field. The leatherwork for a double bridle is different to that of the snaffle bridle in that a 'slip head' is required to which the second bit attaches.

## THE PELHAM BRIDLE

The actual leatherwork in a pelham bridle is nearly always the same as in a 'normal' snaffle bridle; however, the effect of the bit is different in that it has a lever action, giving a degree of

poll pressure. It is a combination of the curb and bridoon on one mouthpiece, to the cheek of which are attached the bridoon and curb reins, thus trying to make the one bit perform the duties of two. In principle this is not a sound policy, but the fact remains that some horses will go better in a pelham than anything else, particularly strong-pulling horses – obviously it is a stronger bit than any of the more commonly used snaffle family of bits and this is precisely why it is useful, in that it provides more control.

The pelham is frequently used in the show-ring when it is compulsory for a two-reined bridle to be used. It can be used on a horse which has too small a mouth for a double bridle. The vulcanite pelham is popular with many people and can be used with two reins or with a 'D' attachment; the curb chain can be of leather or elastic, or be chain-linked, and will of course have a relatively different effect on different horses and according to which bit it is fitted. It is often necessary to experiment with several bits before purchasing one for an individual horse or pony. Many of the old pelham and Weymouth curb bits are severe and are now out of fashion, especially if they have a 'port'. For a horse or pony that starts to become too strong in the bit he usually wears, it is sometimes worth trying a softer bit; a stronger one may make him fight even more.

The pelham bit and bridle on p58 (bottom right) has a third strap running from the bit and over the poll. This is not the same as the normal bridle required for a pelham. The third strap

is added to make it look more like a double bridle with the extra 'slip head'. This is not essential and is only added for the purpose of showing.

## NOSEBANDS

There are four types of noseband in popular use nowadays: the cavesson, the flash, the grakle, and the drop noseband.

The *cavesson noseband* (see p58, below) is a single strap of leather, and its thickness can vary to suit the animal – for example, wide and plain for a hunter, narrow and perhaps with stitched decoration for a pony. It should be fitted so as to allow two fingers in front of the nose; in height it should lie between the corner of the mouth and the bottom of the mandible (cheek bone).

A *flash noseband* (above left) is generally used to stop the horse opening his mouth; it is correctly fitted if both the cavesson and the drop are done up quite tightly. A *standing martingale* can then be fitted to the cavesson.

A *grakle noseband* (p58, above) will stop the horse from crossing its jaw, but it cannot take a standing martingale. The running martingale in the same photo is fitted correctly, and is being used with martingale stops.

A *drop noseband* has really been superseded by the flash and the grakle.

## MARTINGALES

The martingales most commonly used today are the standing and the running martingales; in racing circles the Irish martingale is quite often seen.

The proper use for a *standing martingale* (above left) is to help control a horse which shakes and throws its head around; it is not simply to hold its head down. It can be attached to a cavesson noseband, the cavesson part of a flash, but never to a drop noseband or a grakle. To fit it, when the horse's head is up and in the correct position for moving, the noseband end of the attached martingale should just reach into the gullet.

The *running martingale* is used to prevent the pony carrying its head above the angle of control.

Ring-ended reins are ideal for use with a running martingale as martingale stops are not needed, since there is no chance of the martingale rings becoming entangled with the reins by the bit. There is also a *bib running martingale* (above right) which helps the rider to stop, and also prevents the horse evading by raising its head above the level where the bit is effective. It offers more control than a plain running martingale. These martingales are used mainly in racing stables when exercising racehorses, but they are also much safer on young horses that may have a habit of trying to take the reins or martingale in their mouths, when a very nasty accident could occur – there is a high risk of them rearing over backwards, something which I have witnessed on several occasions.

The *Irish martingale* consists of two rings connected by a strap about 6in (15cm) long; the reins are passed through the rings. It is to prevent the reins from flipping over the pony's head in the event of a fall.

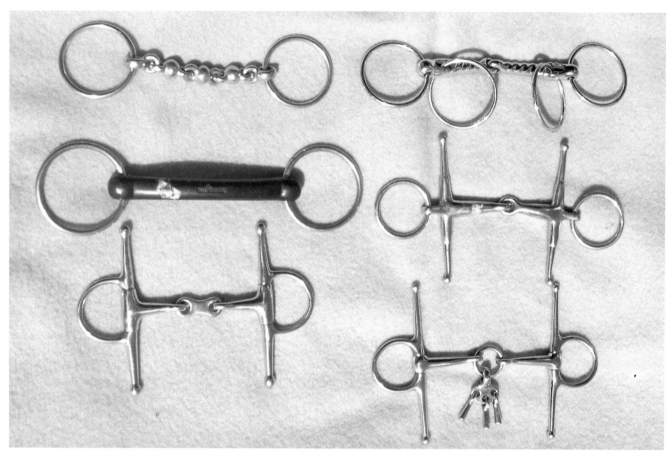

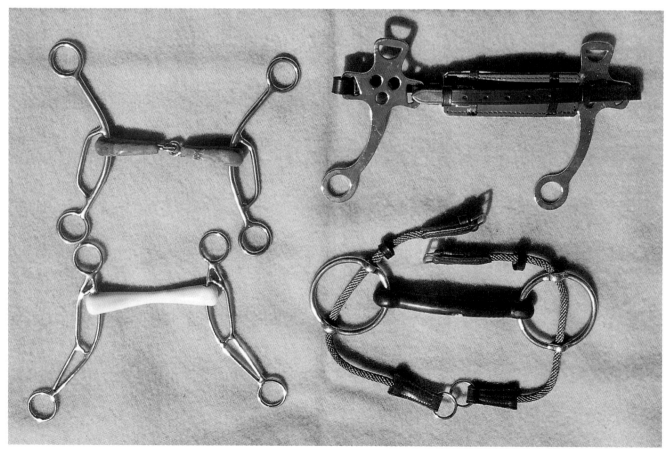

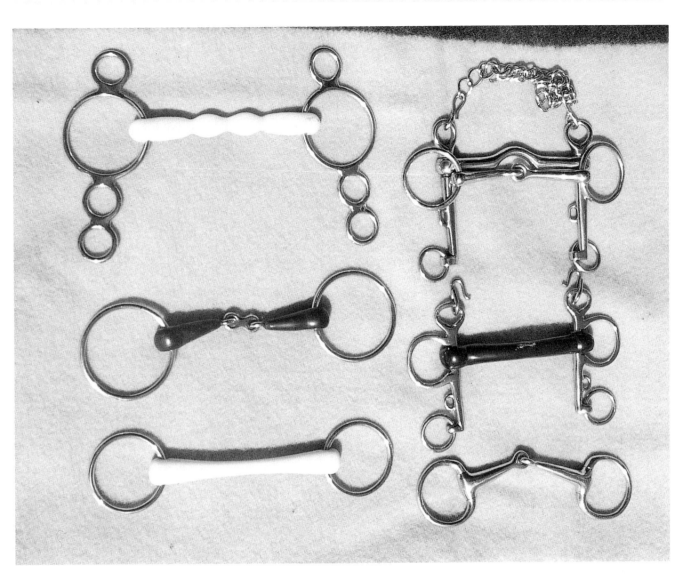

There are numerous bits on the market, each designed to have a different effect. Bitting is a complex subject and if you are in any doubt about which to choose for your horse, seek experienced advice. Making the wrong choice could have disastrous results. The bits illustrated on these pages represent just a small selection of those available.

(opposite above, clockwise from top right) Jointed Scourier bit: this is a relatively severe bit; the double rings prevent the whole thing pulling through the horse's mouth if he is hard to turn.
Eggbutt jointed snaffle with cheekpieces: the elongated bit and loose-ring bit-ring minimise the risk of it pinching.
Jointed snaffle with cheekpieces and key-ring; used for 'mouthing' a young horse. This sort of bit has lost popularity, and is used far less than it used

to be when starting a young horse.
Eggbutt snaffle with French link and cheekpieces; the double joint encourages the horse to 'play' with the bit, although some horses do find its action sharper than the single jointed snaffle. Long cheekpieces, as on three of the bits shown here, stop the bit sliding through the mouth and so are more helpful in turning should a stronger rein contact be needed.
Rubber straightbar snaffle: a very mild but indeed; many people start their young horse in a rubber straightbar, and it is often used successfully with horses that are fussy in the mouth, or have problems with contact.
Waterford snaffle.

(opposite below, clockwise from top right) English hackamore.
Rubber gag: the action of a gag is on the corners of the lips so its effect is powerful. It works well on horses which

carry their head very low and which are difficult to pick up in front of a fence.
Nylon straightbar snaffle and a vulcanite jointed snaffle. The longer, curved cheekpieces make these relatively mild bits more effective when turning and stopping because they provide increased leverage on the poll, in similar fashion to a hackamore.

(above, clockwise fron top right)
Double bridle.
Vulcanite pelham, a favourite bit for a strong horse.
Plain eggbutt jointed snaffle.
Nylon straightbar.
Vulcanite snaffle with French link.
Nylon 'happy mouth' straightbar – the long cheekpieces offer different degrees of leverage, helpful if you need to stop or turn more quickly. This and the two preceding bits are variations on the loose-ring snaffle.

## IN-HAND BRIDLES

The variety of in-hand bridles for showing can be confusing and it is often best to find out what is most suitable by going to a county show and observing what the winners are wearing. Double bridles, however, are used for hunters, ponies and hacks. Youngsters use a showing snaffle bridle but they should always be taught to wear it at home so that they feel comfortable with it before an event. Foals should be shown in a smart leather or white webbing slip, with a webbing lead-rein. Arab types with 'refined' heads often wear a fine headstall. It is important to remember that each breed class requires a correct type of in-hand bridle.

## BITLESS BRIDLES

The *hackamore* (right) is a special type of bitless bridle, particularly useful for a horse which has a spoiled, damaged or otherwise difficult mouth resulting in its being unable to accept a normal bit. It can be a solution to various problems such as teething youngsters, soreness, injury or disease which would make wearing a bit painful or uncomfortable. Leverage acts with strong pressure on the nose and jaw and it must be remembered that the area of the nose to which it applies pressure is just as sensitive as the areas in the mouth to which a conventional bit applies pressure. Careful use of a hackamore can be of great benefit; incorrectly used it may cause damage to the nose area. It is made up of an ordinary headpiece with cheek pieces and throat latch, with a padded nose piece fitted to the lower halves of the two cheek pieces. The reins are fastened to the bottom of the cheeks and when used a significant pressure is felt on the nose.

The hackamore is a familiar sight in the jumping ring where control on turning is essential. It should be used only by an experienced rider, as an inexperienced one may apply too much pressure to the horse's nose. The hackamore is not acceptable in the dressage arena or show-ring.

## HEADCOLLARS, HALTERS AND LEAD-ROPES

A headcollar is a basic necessity for all horses, whatever it is made of. It is used as a method of control and/or constraint, for leading the horse out or just tying him in the stable. The horse should learn from an early age to respect the headcollar, and not to run away from it or pull against it. Competition and show horses must accept being tied up for a long while, without panicking or becoming restless.

The headcollar is simply a bitless version of a bridle, although most are used without browbands. They can be made of various materials, although personally I prefer the quality leather headcollar; the best types have adjustable buckles on the throat latch, noseband and head-piece. Nylon web collars are stronger and cheaper to buy, which makes them a popular choice with most people. These web collars are easily washable, but it should be remembered that nylon can be harsh, and if left on for a long time, the coat and skin can be rubbed sore. Leather headcollars do need attention: regular oiling and soaping is necessary to keep them supple, and stitching should also be checked regularly, in case of it becoming rotten.

A halter is an all-in-one headcollar and lead-rope made of cotton, webbing or rope. Halters are cheaper than the seperate collar and rope, but they are not as widely used. In the show-ring white web halters are used to show foals, usually of the heavier breeds. The main disadvantage of the halter is that the horse cannot be left with a halter on untied in the stable or field.

Lead-ropes are fairly standard, with a spring clip or trigger clip fitted at the end; trigger clips are safer than spring slips as the latter have been known to catch the horse's lip. Ropes are made of cotton or jute, though cotton is more widely used as jute is rough on the hands, even though jute *is* more hard-wearing. For everyday general use ropes can be made easily by plaiting strands of nylon baler twine, attaching a bigger clip to the top.

It is important that the headcollar or halter should be fitted correctly to prevent it rubbing or the horse slipping it off. The headcollar should be tight enough, but comfortable to wear without putting excess pressure around the head.

## SADDLES

There are various types of saddle on the market today: let us start with the *dressage saddle* (1) which is made of leather, its main characteristic being the fact that it has no thigh rolls so the rider's leg can be as free and unrestricted as possible. Also typical of this saddle are the long girth straps to which is attached the 'Lonsdale' girth; thus the buckles lie below the rider's leg and do not interfere in any way with the contact between his leg and the horse's side. The *showing saddle* (2 and 5) is designed with a very straight-cut saddle flap to allow the shoulder of the horse as much freedom as possible.

There are various styles of show/dressage saddle (6); this one is used with a black sheepskin-type material numnah. The white 'lampwick' girth is a good general purpose girth which will stay soft for a long time; it is also hard-wearing, easy to wash, and will only rarely give a horse girth galls, when insufficiently washed.

Probably the most universally used is the *general purpose saddle* (3) which may be adequately employed for all disciplines; it is ideal for the one-horse owner who likes to do a bit of everything. Then there is the *jumping saddle* (4) which is more forward cut so that when the rider's stirrups are at his normal jumping length, his knees will rest on the knee rolls.

There are also linen-lined saddles (see page 56) which are ideal for shows and hunting; they should be sponged clean after use, and can be used on many horses without their having to wear a numnah too.

## SADDLE SAVERS

Various attachments are available to fit on most saddles, such as seat savers; not only will these help to reduce the wear and tear on the seat of the saddle, they will also save wear and tear on the rider's seat! In very wet weather a plastic waterproof saddle cover may be used: these are very good for protecting the leather from becoming over-wet, but be sure that the cover is removed on return to allow the saddle to 'breathe' again.

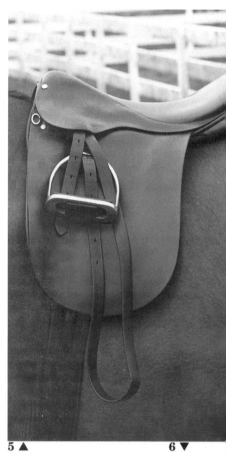

5 ▲       6 ▼

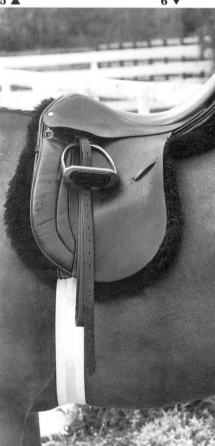

An example of a sheepskin seat saver is shown above.

## SYNTHETIC SADDLES

A relatively new innovation but now seen quite widely is the 'Wintex' or synthetic saddle (right): these are quite hard-wearing, easy to clean, and available for all disciplines. They are much cheaper than a leather saddle, though take care to ensure that a saddle fits correctly before buying.

## WESTERN SADDLE

The Western saddle (left) was designed and redesigned over hundreds of years for practicability, comfort and versatility, since a cowboy has always needed a saddle to fit many horses, and one that would be safe and comfortable to ride in for long hours. A Western saddle rests on the horse's sides more than on its back, so the weight is very evenly distributed. The horn at the front of the saddle is used for mounting and holding on to, and for holding a lasso or length of rope. The stirrups for this sort of saddle are made of wood covered in rawhide; also typical are the many attachments for tying on and carrying equipment and suchlike.

## STOCK-HORSE SADDLE

A stock-horse saddle (right) is commonly used for rounding up animals. Its main characteristic is a deep and very moulded seat so the rider can turn very quickly and sharply without being unseated. Again, there are many attachments for tying on equipment; also a breastplate to help the saddle remain still during rapid changes of pace.

# GIRTHS

Different types of girth are designed to suit different disciplines and saddles, and are available in most tack shops. For example, the girths used on dressage saddles are characteristically short, and usually called either a *Lonsdale* or a *dressage girth*. They are commonly used with an *additional strap* which attaches to the saddle and lies over the girth. Then there is the *nylon string girth* with webbing stays at intervals; this type of girth is commonly seen used on ponies. Although fairly serviceable, great care must be taken to avoid pinching; also, this type of girth may be prone to curling along its length, making it thin and a little uncomfortable.

*Atherstone girths* come in several different designs: they may be plain (second from right in photo); canvas (third from right); or they may have an elastic insert, to be fitted on the left side – this is an excellent girth for hunting or trekking, for example, as it is very hard-wearing and is fairly non-slip; the elastic insert means that it cannot be done up too tight, yet because of this 'give' in it, it fits very closely to the horse. Its care will be the same as for all other leather wear. An Atherstone made of canvas webbing (sixth from the left) will be cheaper and less likely to cause girth galls or rubs in a soft-skinned horse; again, the elastic insert will add to the comfort of the horse. A good general purpose girth is available made of a webbing-type material; the one illustrated (fourth from right) unusually has a loose girth-strap attachment; this design is most helpful on saddles with uneven holes. Finally there is the very popular *Cottage Craft girth* (first on right) which is easy to clean, cheap compared to a leather girth, and very soft.

From the left: two Lonsdale, or dressage, girths; strap which lies over a dressage girth; nylon string girth; two Atherstone girths; a general purpose girth, then two more Atherstones; finally the universally popular 'Cottage Craft' girth.

# BOOTS AND BANDAGES

## BRUSHING BOOTS

These are used in order to prevent damage to the legs should either one knock against each other; the boot with three straps is used on a pony's front legs, the four-strap being used on a horse's front legs or a pony's hind legs, the five-strap being for a horse's hind legs. The examples shown are made of a neoprene-type material with velcro straps, with a tougher, plastic-type material on easily rubbed areas. They should always be fitted with the straps facing to the back when done up. They may be cleaned using soap and water and a stiff brush. In order to keep the velcro sticky it is necessary to remove all hair, bits of straw and so on regularly.

Brushing boots are usually worn for jumping, cross-country or fast work. They are not permitted in dressage and pure showing classes. New regulations now allow the use of brushing boots in the jumping phase of working hunter classes but they should be removed for the conformation and second phase. Only plain-coloured and simple boots should be used in the ring.

## OVER-REACH BOOTS

The white rubber, bell over-reach boots illustrated are used to prevent damage from the hind hoof should it strike into the heel of the front hoof. Although they are cheap to buy, they have several drawbacks: they can be very difficult to put on and get off; it is not advisable to use them in heavy going as they tend to act like plungers and make it harder for the horse to lift its feet out of the mud; and in heavy going they readily turn inside-out, when they provide no protection at all. They do not have a long life as they tear easily. Scrub with hot water to clean.

With the continuing problem of these boots turning upwards and inside out, the 'Westropp' petal boots are an alternative. They consist of a number of overlapping leaves or petals of tough synthetic material. These are threaded on to a plastic strap which has a buckle fastening around the pastern. These boots are more expensive, but each petal can be replaced if damaged or torn, or extra petals can be added if a larger-sized boot is required. These boots are far superior to the less expensive standard sort. Care should be taken to ensure that the pastern is not rubbed by the plastic strap.

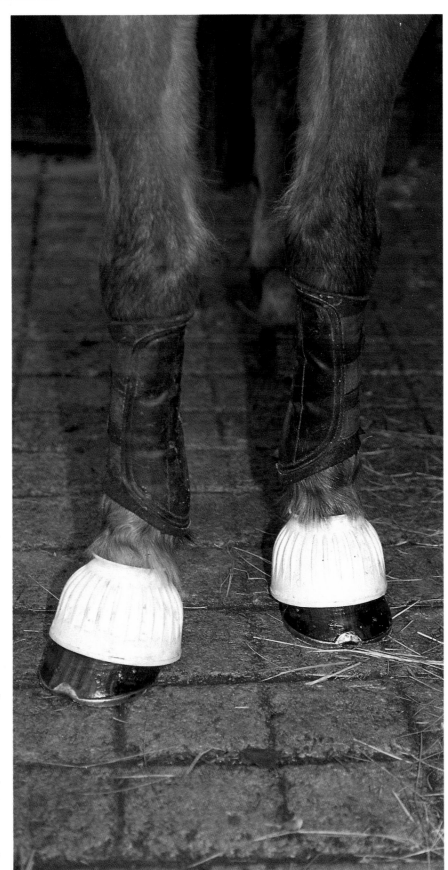

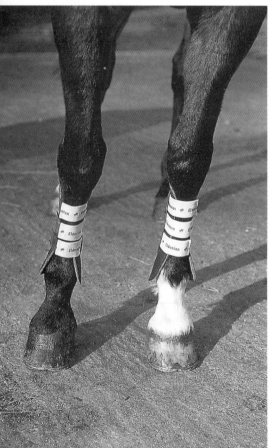

## TENDON BOOTS

Open-fronted tendon boots protect the back of the leg from impact wounds; the ones in the illustration (left) are made of a foam-rubber type substance with velcro straps across the front of the leg. They can also be made of plastic (below left), as these are shaped on the inside to give added support and so they 'mould' to the tendons. This open-fronted variety is commonly used by show jumpers because if a horse hits a fence, it will obviously feel the impact and should 'pick up' a little more next time. The plastic boots are very easy to clean – just use soap and hot water and they will clean up as new every time. This type of manmade fibre is excellent as it does not hold water and will therefore dry easily and quickly. Like all leg boots of this type, they must be securely fitted in order to prevent them from falling down.

## KNEE BOOTS

Knee boots should be worn at all times on the road and are equally advisable when riding on hard or stony ground where a horse may slip. They must be fitted with the top strap snugly around the top of the knee so that they cannot fall down over the joint, and the bottom strap fitted loosely so the joint can move freely. Care of the leather-work of this type of boot is the same as for other leather-work; the felt parts may be cleaned carefully with soap and water.

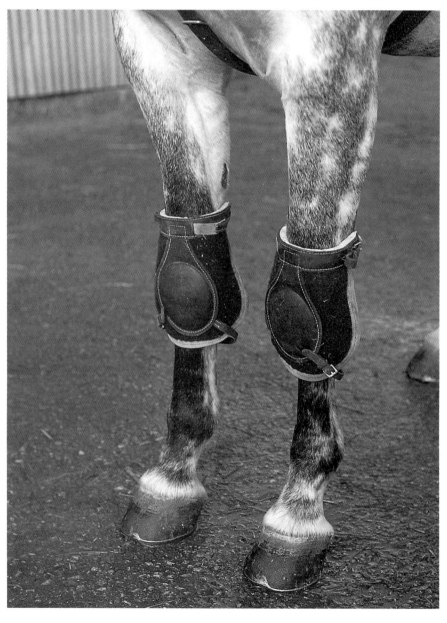

## BANDAGES

Exercise bandages should cover the leg from below the knee – without restricting the joint – to just above the fetlock joint. Not only will they help to prevent strain on the tendons, they will also reduce the risk of injury to the leg through brushing-type injuries. The ones illustrated have velcro tapes to secure them, but ordinary tie bandages are also available. When applying this type of bandage, care must always be taken to ensure that the tapes are not tied or secured on the back or the inside of the leg, where they might interfere with the movement of the tendons; ideally they should be secured towards the top of the leg on the outside. Many people like to put a correctly fitted piece of gamgee underneath the bandage, as extra comfort for the horse. It is important to get to know your bandages by practising several times – particularly if they are new ones – in order to find out how long they are, and therefore where to start bandaging so as to be sure that the tapes end up in the right place.

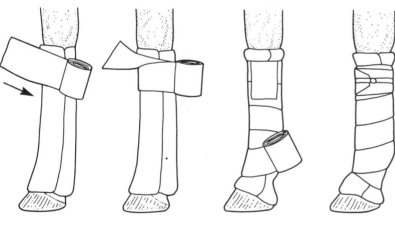

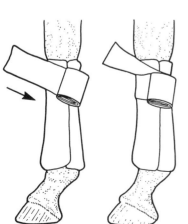
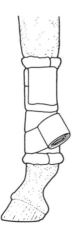

**PUTTING ON BANDAGES**

a) **Stable/travelling bandages.** Wrap your padding smoothly around the leg (damping the hair slightly helps keep it in place), and learn the trick of holding it on whilst applying the bandage. There are various methods, and this one is as effective as any. Leave a little end of bandage free and place it across the leg as shown. Take a turn around the leg and let the end drop down. You can now either bandage over the end, or leave it free as you bandage down the leg. You should aim to cover half the previous turn each time. Take the bandage well down under the fetlock to the heel, where it will take a natural turn upwards, and bandage back up again. Cover the free end (if not done before) and tie the (smooth) tapes only as tightly as the bandage. Finish in a firm bow and tuck the ends in. If possible, cover the bow by turning down a fold of bandage over it

b) **Exercise bandages** are put on in essentially the same way, but they do not normally go below the fetlock joint as this would interfere with the horse's action. However, some competition horses have their bandages applied well down round the fetlock, ostensibly for extra protection

# HORSE CLOTHING

Nowadays in all our tack shops there is a wide selection of rugs and rug accessories, and the choice is often baffling. It is possible to pay well in excess of £100 for a rug, though the cheaper ones may be only £20, depending on the type of rug required. The following sequence of photos illustrates a selection of the more useful, and probably more commonly used, items of horse clothing.

## OUTDOOR RUGS

A horse turned out in a *New Zealand rug* can be sure to stay clean, warm and dry, since this design has a waterproof outer covering and is lined with a warm fleece. However, care must be taken to fit it correctly, to minimise the chance of it coming loose and slipping, causing discomfort and the risk of entanglement. The rug pictured has two strong leather buckles at the front, and cross-over leg-straps at the back. Correctly fitted, the rug should not move very much; it should be well pulled forwards to make sure it does not dig into the horse's neck at the front. Cross-over surcingles on any New Zealand rug must be done up snugly around the horse – a hand's width between surcingle and horse is the recommended fitting – and not dangling as a horse that is rolling may become entangled and then panic, at grave risk to itself.

The new-style modern Masta rug (opposite above) is an excellent all-year-round *turn-out rug*; the outer covering is made of special anti-rip fabric, and the inside is a cellular anti-sweat fabric to help prevent sweating up in the warmer months. This make of rug is an excellent choice as they all seem to fit better than other rugs.

The photo opposite below shows an Australian *protection sheet/outdoor rug*: although they look precarious in their fit and as if liable to slip, in fact they rarely seem to do so; and often a rug is individually made. This is a cotton flax mixture which is shower-proof; it has an individual neck protector and a tailguard. This type of rug will protect from heat, flies and tropical storms in the daytime. Rugs such as these are usually much deeper than those in the UK.

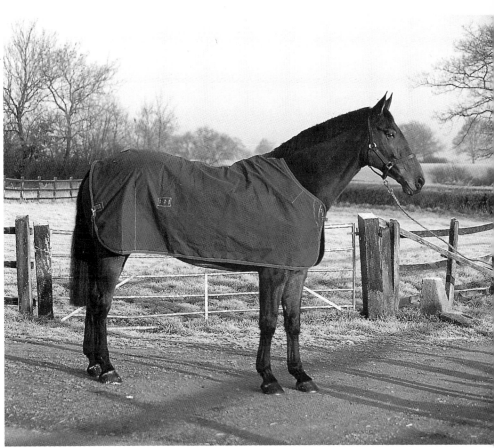

## STABLE AND EXERCISE RUGS

The *stable rug* comes in a huge variety of types. One example is a quilted nylon rug with different thicknesses of filling. The quilted rug is designed to keep the horse warm in cold weather. The best type has a heavy-weight nylon outer and a cotton inner lining with a thermo-insulated filling. Blankets may be required underneath these depending on the horse and weather conditions. Jute rugs with a woollen lining are not so commonly used with clipped or thin-skinned animals as they tend not to be warm enough and require extra blankets.

The *woollen day-rug* is ideal for use in the day or for travelling and so forth. The one pictured is very well fitted to its wearer, though ideally will be used with a roller. This is an excellent example of the depth a rug should be for use in the stable.

In hot weather *cotton summer sheets* can be used to keep flies off and maintain a clean dust-free coat. These

sheets will not cause sweating and will let moisture escape easily.

Summer sheets can also be used to protect the lining of night rugs, especially when the horse is shedding its coat. When using blankets with stable rugs, the addition of a cotton sheet will help to stop the blanket from slipping back as well as keeping the coat looking smooth under a heavier rug.

The ultimate in rug technology must be the *Insulux rug*, as it has the unique property of being able to keep a horse warm in cool weather and cool in hot weather. The fabric 'Insulux' has a layer of air pockets in it so the horse may be kept comfortable in all weathers. In fact, the rug illustrated is a little too small all round for this horse – it should be deeper and longer; however, the cross surcingles will keep it secure at all times. This is the rug most commonly used by the majority of competition horses when travelling, both in the UK and elsewhere; moreover the combination of colours can be varied to suit the individual owner or stable.

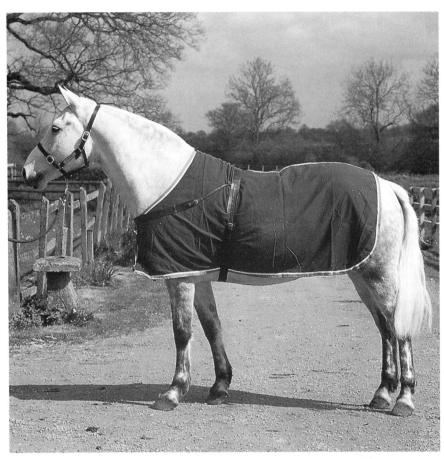

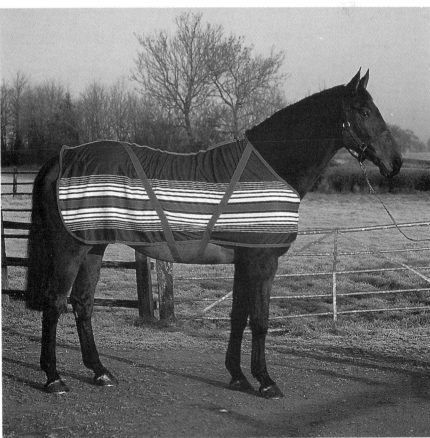

A *woollen exercise rug* is commonly used under a saddle when a horse goes out on exercise; it will help to keep a clipped horse's back warm on a very cold day. It is important that a rug such as this is not too big, otherwise it will flap around and may frighten the animal. A fillet string is usually attached to the rug at the back to keep it down over the horse's quarters.

The *anti-sweat rug* is commonly used on a sweating or wet horse to help it cool down and dry off; the holes allow the air to circulate and therefore the horse to cool slowly, thus reducing the risk of chill. This type of rug *must* be used with a roller to stop it slipping, and it must be used in conjunction with another rug put on top of the sweat rug, to aid the drying process. Note that it is important to store an anti-sweat rug folded up, because if hung as it would be on the horse it would stretch and become so deep it would be dangerous.

## HOODS

When fitting any hood, care should always be taken that it does not rub or damage the eye; this is particularly important when fitting a stable hood. Many long hoods now have fitments which attach them either to the rug or the roller, and this of course prevents them slipping forwards or over the horse's eye. Three types of hood are illustrated here: first, a long woollen sort that was commonly used when travelling a horse – and still is now if it feels the cold. Secondly, an *exercise hood* which is worn underneath a bridle and is commonly used on a fully clipped-out horse or for keeping an ill horse warm when exercising it in hand. Fitted properly, the hood allows good vision and is not tight around the throat area. And finally another long hood, commonly used to keep the horse warm and clean in the stable at night; it may also be put on when a horse is turned out in his New Zealand. Special care must be taken to make sure that the hood will stay down securely over the horse's shoulders. In the USA and Australia, hoods are commonly used to prevent flies becoming a problem; also the hot sun in these areas may burn the coat and change its colour.

Hoods are best washed by hand using a mild detergent, or in warm soapy water.

## FLY FRINGES

Fly fringes, and the ear cover plus fly fringe combined, are generally made of cotton, and are attached with ties to the halter or bridle. They protect against flies and midges: many horses are extremely sensitive to any flying insects, and will fuss their heads about in reaction; in a competition this can seriously affect their concentration and so also their performance. Fly fringes are allowed in show-jumping competitions, but are not permitted in either official dressage or horse trials. To clean: wash in warm, soapy water.

## STORING RUGS AND BLANKETS

Rugs and blankets may be stored in trunks whilst not in use, a practice which is fine as long as they are checked regularly to see that nothing is nesting in the trunk! Alternatively shelves can be used to store rugs, an excellent system as rugs and clothing are easily accessible and a particular compartment or shelf may be labelled with a certain horse's name so all its belongings may be kept together. Also available now are rug 'wardrobes': these consist of a large metal frame with several sections so that many rugs may all be hung together for drying or storing, but taking up as little space as possible.

# 4
# FEEDING

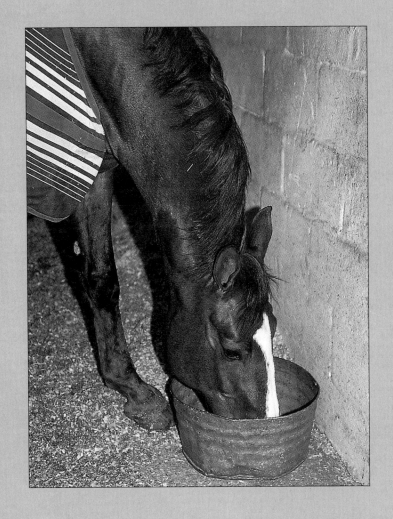

Concentrate Feeds  81
Forage  86
Horses Living Out  87

The feeding of horses, whether it be one or many, is an art which can only be acquired by careful observation and attention to detail. It cannot be learned from books alone, only from practical experience. A horse's diet may be divided into two categories: bulk food and concentrates. Hay or haylage is the bulk food, concentrates include, basically, manufactured feeds, oats, barley, maize and linseed. Every effort should be made to become a good feeder, that is, to understand the nutritive value of the various concentrate feeds, and their benefit/necessity in relation to the horse or pony. There are no hard and fast rules as to how much hay and corn a horse should or should not have – each must be treated as an individual, and to over-feed and under work is just as bad as to under-feed and over-work. Breeding and conformation will also have an effect on a horse's ability to carry condition; for example a tall, long-backed narrow horse will never carry weight or look as well as a short-backed, deep-bodied horse – the cobbier sort of animal will always be much easier to keep weight on than the quality type.

In winter, horses in light work will require good hay, possibly *ad lib* if they are not gross in condition, but only a minimum of concentrates; whereas the hunter working regularly will require anything from 10 to 20lb (4.5 to 9kg) of concentrates, plus good hay to maintain his condition throughout the hunting season. Stabled ponies vary greatly as to their feeding needs, as the risk of over-feeding is very great. Bad doers and shy feeders will probably require extra small feeds during the day, and a last feed at night is always beneficial. Try to find out their likes and dislikes – it can help to add tempters such as carrots, apples and molasses to the feed, to keep them eating and so prevent them losing condition.

In the feeding of concentrates, a balance must always be maintained between the ration and the amount of work the horse is doing; thus concentrates should be altered only when the horse is fitter and he is doing more work, rather than feeding excess concentrates when it is not necessary. Thus for a hunt horse which has just come off grass, the concentrate ration should be started very lightly – perhaps 2–3lb (1–1.4kg) each of oats and a coarse mix or cubes – and the ration increased daily until the animal is in full work (see box on page 80).

Horses should be fed little and often; some people advocate four, even five feeds per day, although this system often proves difficult to fit in to many stable routines – it can also interrupt the horse's rest time, which is an important consideration. Nevertheless the horse is very adaptable, and within reason will normally comply with its owner's own schedule if necessary.

Grass is the most natural food for horses, and as long as the quality of herbage is good, can constitute the maintenance diet from spring to autumn. *Beware*, however, with the smaller native type of pony: too much grass in spring and early summer can cause laminitis, a blood condition resulting in pain in the feet, and great distress to the pony; this type must be severely rationed at this time of year if the grass is at all good – five or six hours' grazing per day may well be sufficient. On the other hand, horses stabled during the summer months will certainly benefit from cut grass if it is available – though do not, *on any account*, offer lawn mowings of any type or description because horses will often bolt these, which can cause acute colic and often death.

Good clean water should be available all the time; for stabled horses this might be from a waterbowl, or in two buckets, both checked regularly. The watering of horses out of doors should be taken very seriously as all too often this essential facility is neglected, with dirty containers and a severely reduced supply in times of frost or heatwave. A shallow running stream is ideal, but do be careful to see that all horses are drinking from it. Mains water in a self-filling tank is also good, but of course this must be kept running in bad weather. Always ensure that all containers are safe, and have no dangerous or sharp edges.

## Feed chart for a variety of ponies

| Description | Morning | Midday | Evening |
|---|---|---|---|
| Blood pony | 1 chaff, ½ nuts | 1 nuts (Horse and Pony), 1 chaff | 1 chaff, ½ nuts |
| JA jumper | 2 coarse mix | 1 bran, ½ nuts | 1 bran, ½ nuts |
| Show pony in full work | 1 bran, 1 sugar beet, ½ nuts | ½ chaff, 1 coarse mix | 1 Supa barley, 1 sugar beet |
| Working hunter pony in light work, such as Pony Club activities, hacking etc | 1 oats, 1 nuts, ½ chaff | No midday feed necessary | 1 nuts (Horse and Pony), 1 bran, 1 chaff, ½–1 sugar beet |
| Small fat pony prone to laminitis | No hard feed generally necessary in summer, restrict grazing. Ad lib hay in winter. May have 1 chaff, 1 low protein/energy nuts but according to age and size. | | |

Measurement used is per scoop

## Feed chart for a variety of hunters

| Description | Morning | Midday | Evening |
|---|---|---|---|
| Big, quality TB hunter in full work | 2 oats, 1 coarse mix or nuts, sugar beet to mix | 2 oats, 1 alfa A, 1 chaff, 1 coarse mix, sugar beet | 1 bran, 1 chaff, 2 oats, 1 coarse mix, 1 nuts, ¾ sugar beet |
| Excitable, good eater, but doesn't hold weight | 1½ cooked flaked barley, 1½ Horse and Pony nuts, 1 bran | 1 oats, 1 non-heating mix, 1 Supa barley, ½ non-heating nuts, 1 chaff | 1 bran, 1 chaff, 1 non-heating nuts, 1 coarse mix, 1 Supa barley, 1 oats |
| Fat half-bred | 2 oats, ½ Horse and Pony nuts | No lunch necessary | 2 oats, ½ nuts, ½ chaff, ½ bran, 1 sugar beet |
| Show hunter (showing rations) | 2 oats, 1 nuts or mix, 1 chaff, sugar beet to mix | 2 oats, 1 nuts, 1 mix, 1 chaff, ½ Supa barley | 2 oats, 1 mix, 1 nuts, 1 chaff, 1 Supa barley, 1, sugar beet |

Measurement used is per scoop

Weight per scoop: oats = 2¾lb (1.25 kg)  coarse mix = 2¼lb (1 kg)
micronised barley = 2¾lb (1.25 kg)  cubes = 3¼lb (1.25 kg)

## FEEDING THE SHOW HORSE

• Always feed according to size, age, and the type of work the horse is doing; for example, the big show horse will require a large amount of feed to keep his condition, especially during the season when he must spend long hours away at shows.

• For any stable-kept horse, ad lib hay of the best quality has no equal; this is particularly true for show horses, and all horses kept in hard work who should have plenty of hay – except fat cobby types.

• Generally speaking, oats are good for hunters and horses, but not for wizzy ponies.

• Barley: cooked, flaked barley is good to add condition, Supa barley is excellent to help a horse maintain its weight; it also contains linseed which is excellent for the coat.

• Bran and/or chaff, and sugar beet are used for adding bulk to feeds. Because they are non-heating they are used for excitable horses and ponies, although their nutritive level is low.

• Alfa A is an excellent sort of chaff. It is more nutritious than ordinary chaff and is also good for adding condition; it is especially beneficial for weak and brittle feet.

• Mix and nuts are of great variety: some are made for specific types of horse, eg stud cubes or mix for brood mares, racehorse cubes for horses in fast work, non-heating for excitable or resting horses.

• Additions to the feed (supplements) can be given to help speed up condition or to keep weight on, or just to get a good, shiny, quality coat.

• Boiled barley is good for hunters in winter, and in particular helps a horse gain/maintain its weight and condition.

• Linseed is excellent for giving a bloom to the coat and skin.

• Thrive is a very effective supplement to aid digestion and maintain condition.

• Cod-liver oil in powder or liquid form is an excellent all-round supplement; it is recognised as particularly benefiting the coat and skin.

• Always use feed of the very best quality; oats should be clean not dusty, feed should never, ever look or smell mouldy.

• It is always best to feed regularly: three or even four times a day helps the horse to digest and utilise the feed to the maximum.

# CONCENTRATE FEEDS

## CUBES/NUTS

Cubes or nuts are made from selected foods which are ground up and pelletted. Several different varieties are available and the nutritional value varies according to their type: for example there are horse and pony nuts, racehorse, stud and grass nuts which contain a variety of concentrates to the required protein, fibre and oil levels. Cubes are excellent for feeding out of doors as there is little waste; however, not all horses – especially the fussier feeder – relish them when fed indoors. Other advantages of feeding cubes are that they save storing several different types of feed; it is a very easy system for the owner of one or two horses; and they are an excellent way for the less experienced person to feed, since the different feedstuffs contained therein constitute an already correctly balanced diet. Excellent feeding charts are provided with better known brands of this type of food.

## COARSE MIX

Coarse mixes are now very popular; they also constitute a convenient way of feeding, plus the fact that most horses and ponies relish them. Again, they vary in their content and there is now a mix available for every type of horse. On the whole they contain soya beans, micronised flaked maize and rolled oats and barley, with molasses as an additive, making them very palatable and an altogether most attractive food. It is just as well to check with the manufacturers the feeding requirements of the individual animal, to be sure you are feeding enough of the right sort.

## BRAN

Bran can be used in many different ways when feeding, though nowadays a lot of nonsense is talked about its usefulness. It is an off-product of wheat, but is no longer as nutritious as it used to be because of efficient modern refining methods; all too often it is dusty and of poor quality. Nonetheless for horses that are off work or on a low protein diet it is invaluable, as also for show horses and ponies when fed with sugar beet pulp and chaff. Moreover it is useful for making up a good proportion of the daily bulk necessary to the horse. A bran mash is made by adding boiling water to a bucketful of bran plus a handful of salt (though be careful with the water – the consistency should be crumbly, not sloppy); it should then be allowed to stand and steam. A mash is an excellent feed for a horse which has come home after a hard day's work. It can also be used as a bran foot poultice, for example for a horse with corns or a septic foot.

## ROLLED OATS

Rolled oats used to be the standard feed for the average horse in work, and are the principal feed for racehorses and hunters. They should be clean, light-coloured and dust-free, and only lightly rolled or cracked. Whole oats should not be fed as the horse cannot digest them properly. However, oats have a low calcium-to-phosphorous ratio and are best not fed alone; ideally they should have some form of calcium supplement to balance the roughage. They can also have a considerable 'heating' effect, particularly on ponies.

For stabled horses in full work oats as part of the feed ration are excellent. Horses in fast work or who hunt regularly can have up to 20lb (9kg) a day. Oats are not suitable for small ponies due to their heating effect, whereas older horses can benefit from them in the winter.

## BARLEY

Barley (right) can be fed either as rolled and micronised (cooked) or as boiled, whole grain, and is a fattener, generally offered to horses which do not hold their weight well. Because it is high in starch it must be fed in careful relation to exercise; in particular it can have a 'heating' effect on excitable animals.

## SUGAR BEET PULP

Sugar beet pulp (left) can be in the form of cubes or shredded beet and is a good cheap source of energy and roughage; it can be used to make feeds interesting and given to horses requiring a lot of bulk. If fed in excess it has a highly laxative effect. The small horse should be fed approximately 1–2lb (0.5–1kg) daily and the larger animal 2–4lb (1–1.4kg) (soaked weight). It should be noted that it is absolutely *vital* to soak sugar beet cubes *and* shreds for at least twelve hours, in the proportion of at least double the amount of water to dry matter. The photograph shows sugar beet in cubed form and when soaked.

## CHAFF AND ALFALFA

**Chaff** is hay chopped up very small so it can be added to the horse's concentrate feed, to bulk it up and to prevent the horse bolting it. **Alfalfa** is another form of bulk that can be added to feed; it is made from lucerne and has a higher protein level, and is therefore more useful for many types of horses, especially youngsters and horses in training. It is more expensive to feed alfalfa than chaff, but because it is so much more beneficial it is worth the extra cost.

## SUPPLEMENTS

There are so many different types on the market, for so many different purposes, that the average horse owner may easily become confused with the amount on offer. Generally, however, it is not necessary to add supplements to a horse that is receiving a sufficient, balanced diet, though they can certainly help improve a horse's coat and its general health, particularly as concerns youngstock and horses in strenuous competition work. A traditional and excellent feed supplement is cod liver oil.

A mineral lick should be included in all boxes for the stabled horse.

Herbs are a very useful component in the feeding of horses, but particularly show animals. Fenugreek is excellent for putting on condition and for tempting a fussy feeder; it is high in oil, so will also give the coat a good shine. Rosemary is a good hair conditioner, and improves hair growth: soak a handful in boiling water for a few minutes, then strain and cool – saturate hair, and leave to dry naturally. Certain herbs have a remarkably calming effect on highly strung horses: for example, chamomile tea – tip about half a pint (¼ litre), including flowers, over the evening feed every day.

## MAKING UP FEEDS

The most usual method of mixing and conveying feed is in large plastic buckets as these are easily carried and washed, and cheap to buy. Purpose-made feed scoops are generally used to measure out each portion of food quickly; a 'scoopful' represents a certain weight, and this is an easier alternative to weighing out each feedstuff individually.

## STORAGE BINS

The storing of feed is very important: it should be kept clean and dry, and protected from vermin – all feed can deteriorate if kept in unsuitable conditions. Suitable containers might be in the form of metal bins, old freezers or plastic dustbins; in large establishments metal containers are often used as they hold a considerable quantity of food both safely and conveniently, though they should always be raised off the floor on wooden blocks. The one- or two-horse owner can use plastic dustbins, each holding about one 56lb (25kg) bag of feed; these are quite adequate as protection from rats and mice. When using large containers, however, make sure that the food is all used up to the bottom regularly, otherwise a build-up of stale food will occur.

# FORAGE

Good hay should be a good colour, and the greener the better providing it smells sweetly. Hard seed hays are preferable for horses in hard work, whereas softer meadow hay is more suitable for ponies and horses in light work or resting.

Large round hay bales are ideal for a large yard which has the machinery necessary to handle them, but they are quite impractical for the average small establishment. Hay can be fed loose on the floor, although in a shavings bed this can be very messy and impractical. Haynets are ideal for preventing waste and mess in the bedding, but great care must be taken when tying them up so that they are high enough for animals not to become entangled in them. They are not good for youngstock, which tend to chew and play with them. The metal hayrack is probably the most useful, providing it is not set too high for the size of the horse.

Soaking hay, usually in a barrel or trough, now seems to be a part of every-day stable routine; it certainly seems to lessen the incidence of horses coughing and to reduce respiratory problems, particularly if the hay is of inferior quality. It should be noted that second-class hay should be bought with the intention of soaking, and that even with top-class hay, some horses are better off with it soaked. However, it may only be necessary to damp a haynet to prevent a horse coughing.

**Haylage:** this is a new way of feeding bulk, and is a sort of dry silage; it comes in sealed plastic bags, and has many different trade names. This type of forage is of particular value for horses with respiratory problems; it is also excellent to take to shows and events because the bales are small, compact and tidy. Haylage of different nutritional levels is available, according to the type of horse and the work being done: for example, racehorses will need a high level, laminitic ponies only a very low one. However, it should be noted that this form of forage is very expensive, and can be as much as three times the price of normal meadow hay.

## HORSES LIVING OUT

Horses and ponies should be fed during the winter months, particularly if they are to live outdoors, to supplement the loss of nutritional value in the grass – and it is important to start feeding *before* they start to lose condition. In the case of the mature animal, hay alone may well be sufficient, but young-stock and the more thoroughbred types would need to be fed concentrates. When feeding several horses in the same area, special measures will prob-ably have to be taken to prevent bully-ing: feed vessels should be well apart, for example, and should be of a sub-stantial nature to prevent injury.

Animals living out should always have access to salt and mineral blocks, which can be hung up or kept in a container. There are also various types of feed block on the market specifically made for outside feeding.

When hay is fed in the field it should be left in heaps or wads spaced well apart, and on fresh ground daily; it can also be fed in purpose-made field racks.

It is a good idea to take a long, critical look at your horse, now and again. Is he too fat/thin? Does he look lethargic/bright? Does his coat shine/look dull? Are his feet in good order? If his condition falls short, then you will have to adjust his feed and stable care accordingly.

When you are making your daily checks for injuries, keep a watch for loss of condition, as in winter some horses lose flesh very quickly. The old horse in the picture on the left is in poor condition; his hip bone is just showing and he would need supplementary feeding if kept outdoors during the winter. His neck has become lean and he lacks overall body condition. Older horses often lose condition, even in summer from the heat and flies worrying them; they are better stabled in the day and turned out at night in summer. Compare the condition of this animal with the glossy, healthy-looking animal in the second photograph, showing a good covering of flesh, particularly over the neck and hindquarters.

The sequence of photographs (right) shows three different horses in good condition at different times of the year. Top right: a fit hunter in spring, not carrying a great deal of weight since he was worked all winter, but nonetheless round over his quarters, no ribs showing and a solid neck, and above all a wonderful shine to his coat; you can see from the blanket clip that the darker summer coat is coming through fast. Centre right: in the pink! The height of summer, and the sort of thin-skinned, Thoroughbred type that is very often adversely affected by heat and flies. This one, however, is fit and well muscled up, with a bright eye and plenty of vitality; he has obviously been kept in during the day to prevent him going back. Notice the hoof oil: daily application is an important part of routine management, particularly in dry weather when the hooves will dry out and crack more readily. Bottom right: fat and hairy, on holiday in the winter months, but carrying just the right amount of weight for a cob – lovely and round over quarters and neck but not excessively fat over the ribs. If cobs and half-bred horses are obviously too fat, they will also be carrying too much fat inside, in the heart and arteries, and this will be detrimental to their performance and will put undue strain on lungs and legs. This cob has been kept shod in front: if the hoof quality is poor, and the unshod foot likely to break up, then it is advisable to keep front shoes on even if the horse is resting, his shoes are more likely to stay on for longer when he comes back into work.

## COMPETITION HORSES

Horses need to be both mentally and physically prepared for competitive work, and care must be taken to balance the work : food ration. The race-horse or event horse will be very fit, but a showjumper or show horse needs to carry condition without being too fat.

As horses get very fit they tend to lose their appetites, go off their feed and generally lose their 'sparkle', and great care must be taken to ensure that the individual animal does not lose condition. Weather permitting, a couple of hours out at grass will do them good, and 20 minutes grazing in hand after exercise is also a useful method for settling a horse. A bucket of freshly picked grass is greatly relished by most horses, and can help to revitalise the appetite.

# 5
# GROOMING
# AND
# CLIPPING

Grooming  92
Washing  96
Clipping  98
Pulling the Mane and
    Tail  106
Plaiting the Mane and
    Tail  107

## GROOMING

Grooming is an energetic part of horse care: it keeps the skin in good condition, tones up the horse generally and obviously helps maintain his general appearance. For the stabled horse it can take from ten minutes to one hour, depending on the condition of the horse, the time of the year, and the work that he is being asked to do; thus the clipped-out hunter should have a thorough dressing-over daily, whereas the child's pony may only need a quick brush-off. Horses that are kept at grass do not need daily grooming; if required for riding, a light brush over to remove any mud is all that is necessary – groom too thoroughly and you brush out the natural grease which acts as an extra 'coat' to keep the horse warm and dry if he lives outside. If a horse is hot and damp or sweating after exercise, he is best left to dry, or led out in hand to pick some grass. In some stables, particularly in racing yards, horses are just sponged over after exercise, then left until the evening when they are thoroughly groomed.

Most horses these days do not receive the sort of thorough grooming as was usual in the past when many grooms were employed, with only two or three horses each to do. The amount of time and money now available to the individual has altered the status quo – fewer people have more work to fit into less time, and to resolve this problem some use electric groomers while others prefer to wash and shampoo regularly. Clipping, too, plays an important part in stable management: the long winter coat is removed thus helping prevent undue sweating and so reducing the chore of a great deal of grooming.

The electric groomer is undoubtedly a great help in keeping the stabled horse clean, particularly when it is still in full coat, and does a good job in carefully removing most dirt and grease. These are often used in large stables that have a grooming box, into which horses are led for a thorough grooming. Two types of head are available, with either soft or stiff bristles to cater for the different types of skin and hair. However, take great care to keep manes and tails clear from the rotating brush; tails should always be plaited, and no attempt should be made to use the machine on a horse's head. Also available are smaller electric vacuum

groomers, probably more practical for the small stable and the amateur owner. Horses that are shy of being clipped often benefit from a carefully used electric groomer, though extra care should be taken when introducing a horse to one. Horses groomed with such machines will need to be finished off by hand and given a final wipe over with a stable rubber.

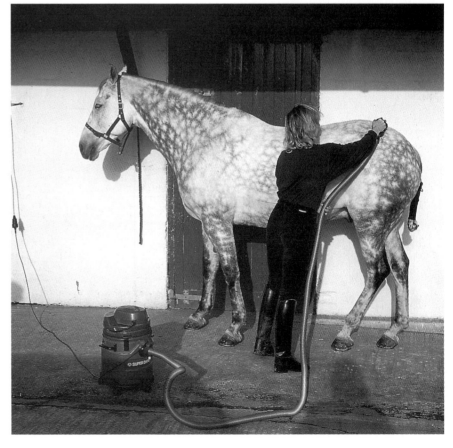

## GROOMING EQUIPMENT

A selection of grooming equipment:
1 **Sponge**: useful for damp-sponge-ing the whole horse and for wiping out eyes and noses; a separate sponge should be kept for docks.
2 **Tail bandage**: put on when grooming is finished.
3 **Dandy brush**: for removing mud and to use on a horse in its full winter coat; it should not be used on a thin-skinned animal or on clipped out areas. Manes can be brushed out with a dandy but not the tail, otherwise too much hair will be pulled out, leaving it thin and straggly.
4 **Rubber curry comb**: for loosening and removing unwanted hair and dirt.
5 **Body brush**: the most important brush of all: use it all over the horse's body and to brush out tails.
6 Soft **dandy brush** or **water brush**: a useful all-rounder.
7 **Metal curry comb**: used with the body brush to remove dirt and grease from the brush.
8 **Plastic curry comb**: to remove dirt and grease from the horse or the brush.
9 **Hoof grease**: supplied with its own brush.
10 **Horse shampoo**.
11 Plastic **sweat scraper**.
12 **Mane comb**: for pulling a mane or tail.

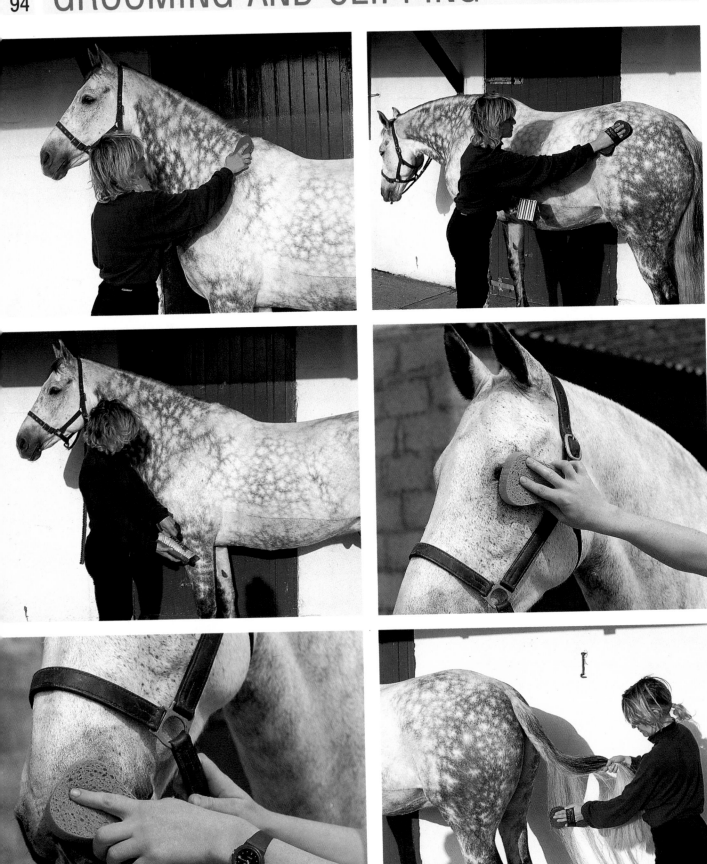

Always tie an animal up for grooming, either with a headcollar and rope, or if it chews a chain can be used. Further, it is always wise to attach a small piece of string to the ring and tie the halter rope to that – then if the horse pulls back the string will break and not the halter, and there will be less risk to the horse. Never tie the horse to a hay rack or manger.

In winter-time a horse that is clipped can have a rug left on his quarters during grooming; in particular this applies to a horse after exercising, when he may still be warm. All mud and sweat can be removed with a dandy brush or rubber curry comb, followed by ten to twenty minutes body brushing depending on the time of day and the condition of the horse. When brushing legs, and in the course of grooming, note any small cuts or abrasions and treat them immediately.

Never attempt to brush a horse's *head* while he is tied up; but remove the headcollar or just put it round his neck. Finally, finish with a good wipe all over his body and legs with a stable rubber, and brush out the mane and tail, dampening the mane to encourage it to lie all over on one side if necessary.

Washing the sheath of a gelding is a part of horse management which is often overlooked. Deep inside the sheath, debris from the skin tends to collect and this can cause the horse discomfort; this area should therefore be washed every couple of months. However, some horses may not approve of you doing this, so take great care that you are not kicked! A mild soap and warm water should be used, with a clean sponge; there are also special solutions that can be bought for this purpose. Strong antiseptics should not be used. Catch hold of the sheath whilst the horse is staling – though be sure that you always do so with tact and patience!

Take particular care of the stabled horse's tail, especially the quality horse with fine hair as too much brushing and separating the hair will in time result in a very thin tail. A fine brush – preferably a soft body brush – should be used *gently*, but only on a relatively clean tail; if in any doubt it is always better to wash it first.

## QUARTER MARKS

For quarter marks on show-ring animals or best-turned-out classes, it is now possible to buy plastic stencils which, when placed on a horse's quarters and brushed over with a wet brush, leave patterned quarters. A damp body sponge can be used to mark quarters making large squares, or shark's teeth on flanks and quarters. A 4in (10cm) square comb can be used to mark the top of the rump. A draught-board effect can be achieved by combing over damp hair in different directions. This gives an added finish to a well turned out horse or may be used for horses in show pony, show hack or riding horse classes.

## CARE OF THE FEET

Last but not least, feet should be picked out and oiled daily both before and after exercise; note also the condition of the shoes. The benefits of hoof oil include helping to prevent the hoof from drying out and cracking; it also adds a finishing touch to the horse's appearance and is an indication of the level of care that has been devoted to him. There are many proprietary brands of hoof oil, and which one you choose is a matter of individual preference.

## TRIMMING HEELS

Fetlock hair may need trimming (see below), and particularly on the commoner type of animal will need to be done with the clipping machine; on the finer, well bred sort it may only be necessary to take surplus hair out with the scissors. When trimming heels with a machine it is usually best not to go up the tendons – this is often unnecessary and can make an animal seem very short of bone. Hair around the coronary band can also be removed to improve appearance.

## WASHING

From time to time it may be preferable to wash the horse or pony from head to toe; there are several reasons for washing:

1 When the horse is finally brought in and stabled, having had a long period out at grass.
2 Prior to clipping right out, as washing will remove all the dirt and grease from the coat and make clipping far easier.
3 Two or three days before a show or event.
4 White or grey horses, as these are always difficult to keep clean.
5 After a skin condition, for example, ringworm and suchlike.
6 After exercise, to make the horse more comfortable and to prevent him breaking out.

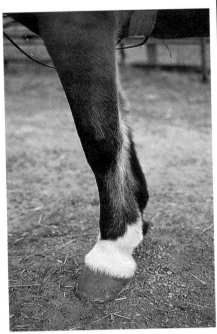

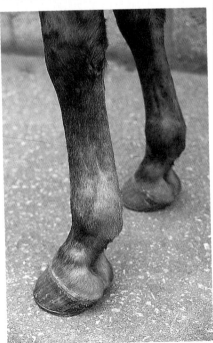

## PROCEDURE

First of all, wet the horse all over, either by hosing if it is quiet and amenable, or with a bucket and sponge. If the weather is hot it can be done outside, though for safety's sake and in winter-time it is best to use a wash-box or a spare stable. Having thoroughly wet the horse, a shampoo should be used; there are many types available, including insecticidal shampoos with additions such as coat conditioners.

After shampooing make sure that all the soap is rinsed out. In cool weather towels should be used to help dry the horse, and a sweat sheet put on to help it dry. Alternatively, if the weather is suitable and the surface correct, the horse can be lunged dry.

In the course of washing, or at any other convenient time, geldings should have their sheath washed out: using a sponge and warm soapy water, wash the whole of the inside of the sheath; afterwards swill out with clean water. Some geldings will need to have a front foot held up by an assistant during this process in order to prevent them fidgeting and kicking. However, they will soon get used to this process.

During the winter, care must be taken to dry the heels after washing otherwise cracked heels and mud fever can develop.

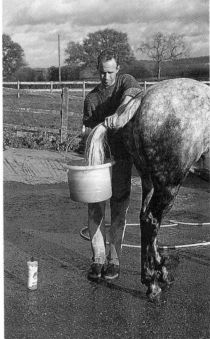

Washing of tails will need to be done carefully so as to avoid being kicked. Therefore, do not rush behind the horse and dip the tail in a bucket of cold water: using warm water and a proprietary shampoo, dip the tail gradually into a bucket and swill round. Using the bottom of the tail, wash the top, then put the bucket down and with two hands work with the hand from top to bottom. Finally, swill thoroughly with a hose, or with warm water with a separate bucket and sponge.

# CLIPPING

During the autumn and winter, horses that are required to work will need part or the whole of their coat removed by clipping. Horses in hard work will need a full clip, for young horses and most ponies a trace clip will be adequate, and there are various styles of clip between these two; although a horse with a long winter coat will probably benefit from being clipped right out.

Before even beginning to clip, be sure that the clippers are in excellent mechanical condition, and that the blades have been re-sharpened even if new. Do not be tempted to over-tighten the blades, as this will lead to severe over-heating of the motor. Once started, never allow the clippers to over-heat – if in doubt, stop and allow them to cool down. In the course of clipping a horse it is important to stop now and again to remove loose hair from the blades, also to apply lubricating oil frequently to ease wear on the blades and motor. There are several well known makes of clippers on the market, which are priced according to their quality and motor size. Great care should be taken of the blades to prevent a broken tooth – one broken tooth can render them useless, and at a cost of approximately £20 plus per set of blades, carelessness can be expensive. For the one-horse owner or the novice it may be advisable to employ someone experienced to do the clipping; the usual cost is from £20 to £40 depending on the style of clip required. Horses in full work – hunting, eventing, racing – will need to be clipped regularly, probably every two or three weeks.

Points to remember when clipping:
1 Approach carefully with clippers.
2 Keep well away from the mane.
3 Be careful not to cut into elbows, flanks or tummy.
4 Never attempt to clip around a twitched nose.
5 Be careful when first trimming the jaw or ears.
6 Never attempt to clip a kicking horse.
7 Never try and clip a wet or a sweating horse.
8 Try to have an assistant handy.
9 Never continue clipping with a hot machine if the clipper over-heats.
10 Always take care of your clipping equipment and send it away to be serviced regularly.

## PROCEDURE

Always let the clippers run for a short while before approaching the horse, so he has a chance to get used to the noise they make; then start quietly near the shoulder. Always clip against the lie of the coat, keeping the clipper head close to the horse. Clip in long strokes, following the lines of the clip of your choice. It is advisable to leave the horse's head until last, and if he is difficult leave the elbows till near the end, too.

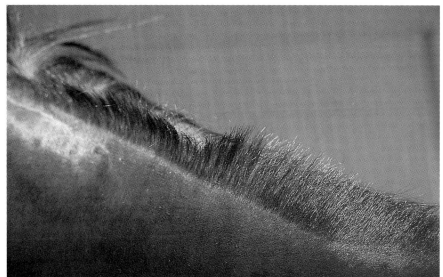

When clipping near the mane, be careful not to get too close – once the mane is cut into it will grow back spiky for the rest of the season. Saddle marks and legs can be marked out with bar soap or tailor's chalk; when doing so, stand close to the horse's side – it is also advisable to have an assistant to hold a front leg up while clipping the hind end.

Starting clipping at the shoulder of a thin-skinned horse with very little coat – not always the easiest sort to do. Care and patience will be required to make a first-class job.

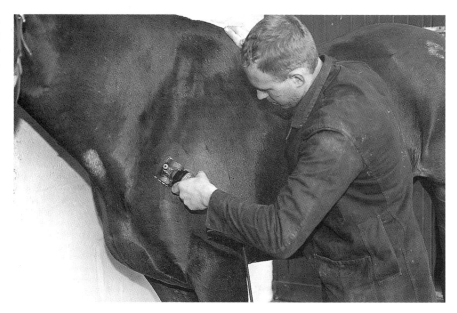

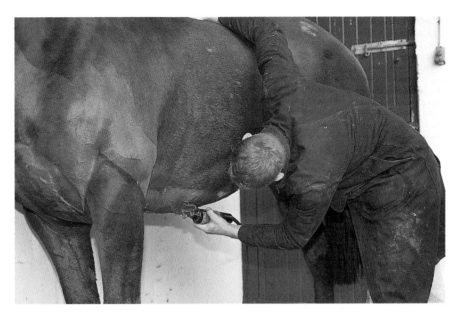

When clipping out the tummy, keep well close to the horse because then the risk of getting kicked will be less.

When marking out the legs, again stand close to the horse.

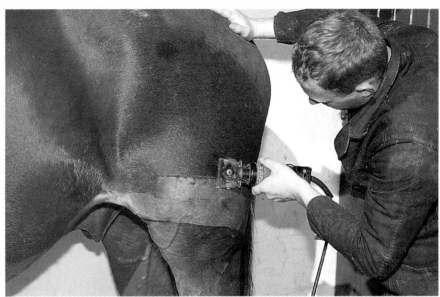

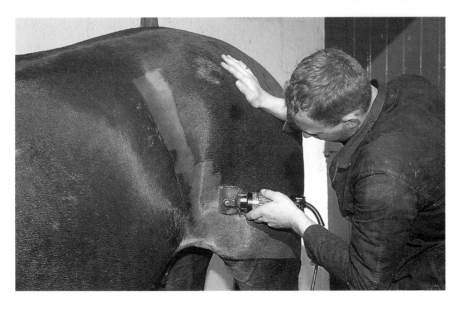

Take great care when clipping out the flank, the sheath area on a gelding or the udder of a mare, so as to avoid cutting into the delicate skin; and it is easier if an assistant draws the front leg forwards when clipping the elbow.

Clipping the sheath area.

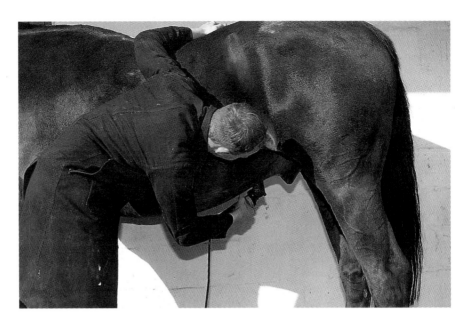

An assistant draws a leg forward so as to facilitate clipping of the elbow area.

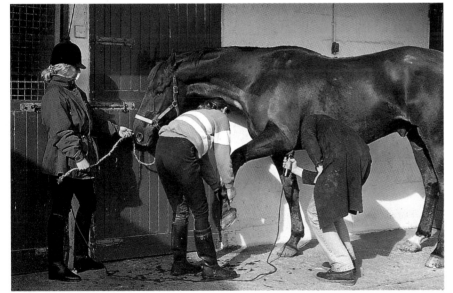

Not all horses like to have their head clipped, or to feel the clippers on their jaw, so care must be taken not to frighten them otherwise they may strike out at the operator with a fore-leg. Some people prefer to leave the inside of the ears, or to trim just their edge.

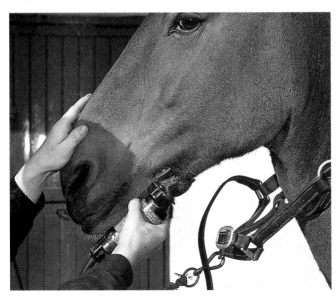

### USING A TWITCH

Difficult horses may need to be restrained with the use of a twitch; this sometimes works wonders, with the horse under complete control. However, never be tempted to trim round the nose of a twitched horse, as should the clippers accidentally touch the stick part, the horse may be quite likely to strike out dangerously with a foreleg. But most horses that would otherwise object, when twitched will allow their ears and head to be clipped out. As an extreme measure sedation may be necessary, for example for a young, nervous, or very difficult horse; however, the veterinary surgeon will be required to perform this, and it should only be done when expert help is at hand.

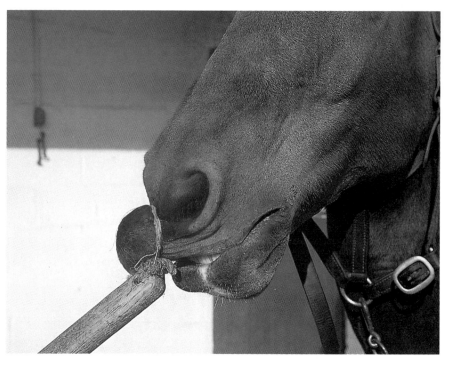

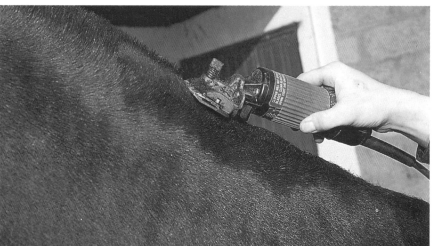

### HOGGING A MANE

Cob-type animals are often better with a hogged mane, and nowadays it is compulsory for show cobs to be hogged; polo ponies also have hogged manes – in fact horses with a thick, strong neck, and particularly the half-bred type, look quite smart hogged. However, horses with a long weak neck will be made to look worse if they have their mane off. And remember that once hogged, a mane will take twelve months to regrow – and even then, some manes will always remain very coarse and untrainable.

To hog a mane correctly, run the clippers straight along the top of the neck, then down each side. Try not to take in more of the horse's coat than is necessary on each side. Once hogged it will be necessary to hog at least every two weeks to remain looking smart.

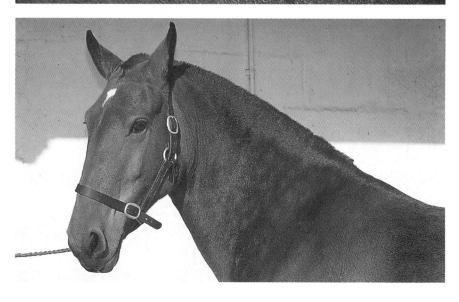

## VARIOUS CLIPPING STYLES

The following photographs show different types of clip to suit the individual horse's work and its owner's requirements.

The belly hair only is removed (above) for a horse during breaking or light hacking, and for children's ponies in the winter holidays. The author is shown here with a four-year-old show hunter in excellent overall condition and well turned out.

A horse with a good trace clip, in excellent condition ready to do any job; this is a practical clip for a horse that perhaps needs to be turned out for a period during the day, also for young horses and children's ponies. This photo was taken of Manuscript shortly after he won the Small Hunter of the Year award at the Horse of the Year Show, and he was regularly hunted with this clip.

Trace clip on a young horse (opposite above); this is a most suitable clip for a youngster during breaking and early training days.

A trace or blanket clip from the rear; the horse has a full unpulled tail.

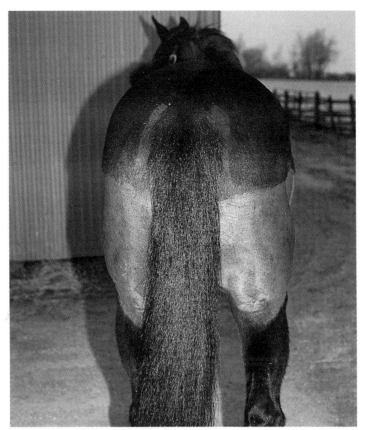

A blanket clip on a fit hunter (opposite below), liked by some as it gives a certain protection to the hindquarters and loin area; it is greatly favoured by the racing fraternity.

A fine example of a fit hunter with a correctly styled hunter clip; note the good slope to the legs and the well-shaped saddle patch. Also the tail which is cut to the correct length, 4in (10cm) below the point of the hock.

# PULLING THE MANE AND TAIL

When pulling a mane, never be tempted to over-pull, ending up with a few spare hairs. This is very easy to do as some animals' manes come out very easily and before you are aware of it the mane is too short. Manes that are pulled too short will never lay down well and tend to sprout upwards. Aim for a neat line along the neck, approximately 4in (10cm) in length.

To pull a mane, comb it out well first, removing any knotted hair. Then, taking a small comb, backcomb the hair up to the roots and pull it out, working your way along the entire neck until the whole mane is of the same length and thickness. Should you have a mane that is very long but also thin, it may not be necessary to pull any hair out or you will end up with no hair at all. This should only require shortening. Using the same backcombing method instead of drawing the hair out, trim the ends off with scissors carefully until you shorten the length of the mane only.

When pulling a tail draw no more than a very few hairs from each side – do not be tempted to rip out too much at a time otherwise when it grows back it will resemble a loo brush! Remember a pulled tail requires regular bandaging to look smart. Always pull a tail over a stable door for safety – this applies to even the quietest of animals.

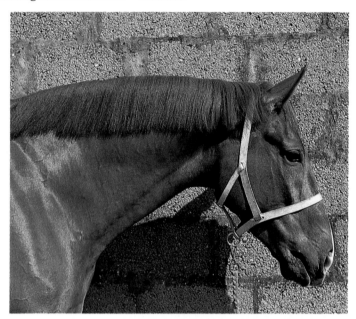

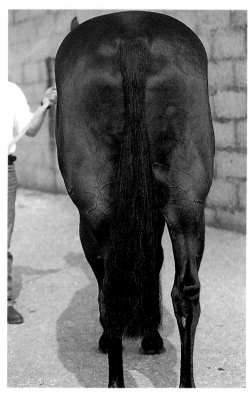

# PLAITING THE MANE AND TAIL

A well-plaited tail looks smart, but needs practice if it is to look perfect. Yearlings and two- and three-year olds usually have their tails plaited in the show-ring. Fine-docked animals plait up well, whereas the more common or coarse or cob-type animals do not. Before even attempting to plait the tail it needs to be well brushed out and perfectly clean; and of course it needs to be a full tail and not previously pulled. The photographs on pages 109–10 provide a step-by-step guide to plaiting the mane and tail.

## WASHING THE MANE

The mane should be washed and shampooed some time before it needs to be plaited, then well brushed out; it is hopeless even attempting to plait a dirty, greasy mane. Ideally it should be 4 to 6in (10–15cm) long.

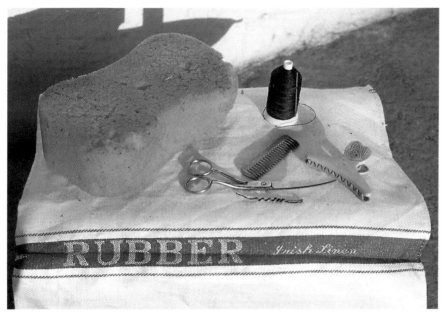

## EQUIPMENT

Before attempting to plait, all materials should be gathered together and are often best kept in a small container of their own.

1 Sponge or soft waterbrush
2 Thread with large needle
3 A pair of sharp scissors
4 Clip

The number of plaits depends on the individual mane and person plaiting, but eight or ten are the usual. Horses with short thick necks look better with small tight plaits, whereas long weak necks can have larger, looser and more upright plaits.

A well-plaited mane with small, neat, tight plaits.

Larger, looser, more upright plaits.

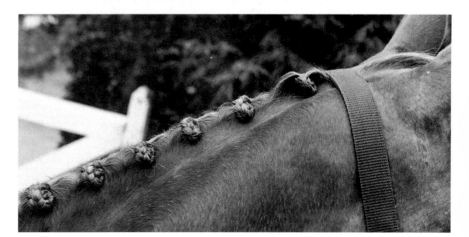

## PROCEDURE

Damp the mane well, take up a section of hair and plait down tightly right to the end (**1**).

**2** and **3** Tie the end of the plait using needle and thread, then take it up to the base of the mane and secure with a stitch or two. Double up and re-stitch.

**4** Stitching up the plait using the cotton, wrapping it tightly around the plait.

**5** Finish by sewing up the mane, rolling the plait up into a tight ball and sewing neatly.

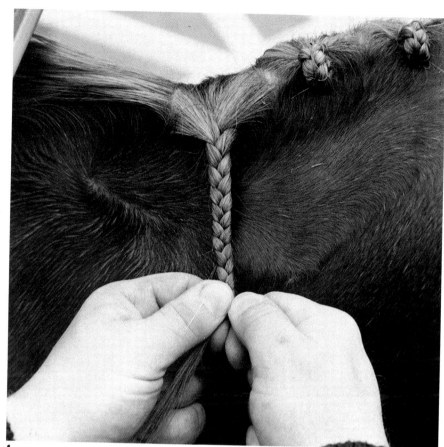

1

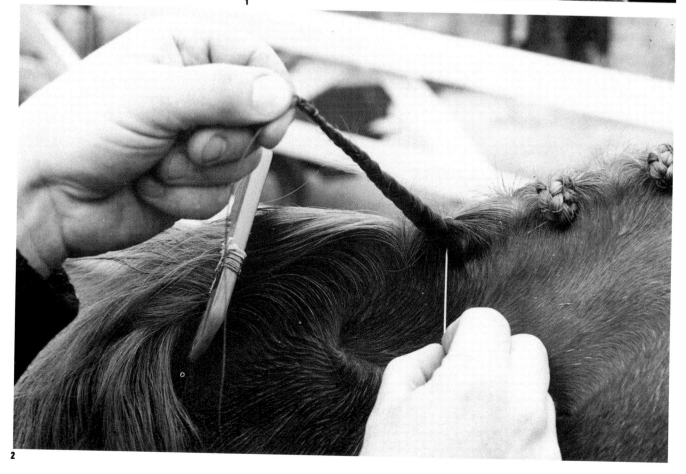

2

3

4

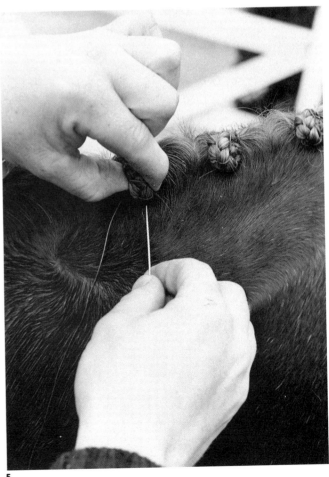

5

## PLAITING THE TAIL

Wet the tail well and take a small section of hair from either side of the tail. With the left hand, pick up a small section of hair from the centre – you should now have three strands of hair with which to start plaiting. Then take a little hair from each side alternately and add this to the plait as you go down the tail. Do not take up too much hair at a time, and keep the plait as tight as possible.

1

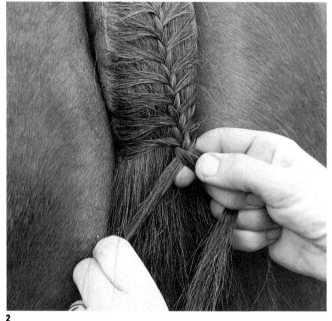

2

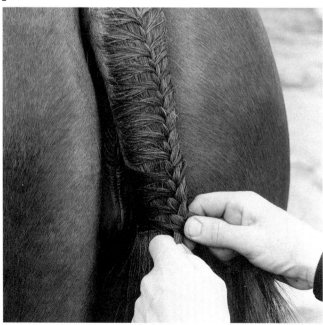

3

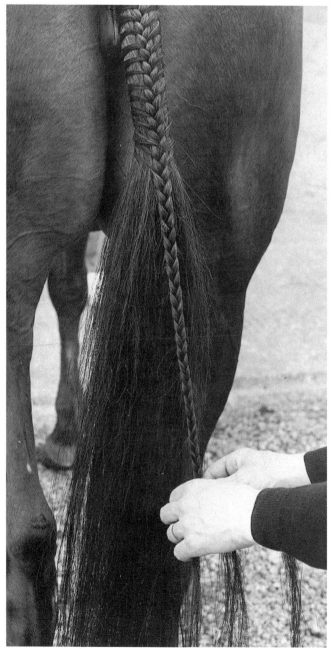

4

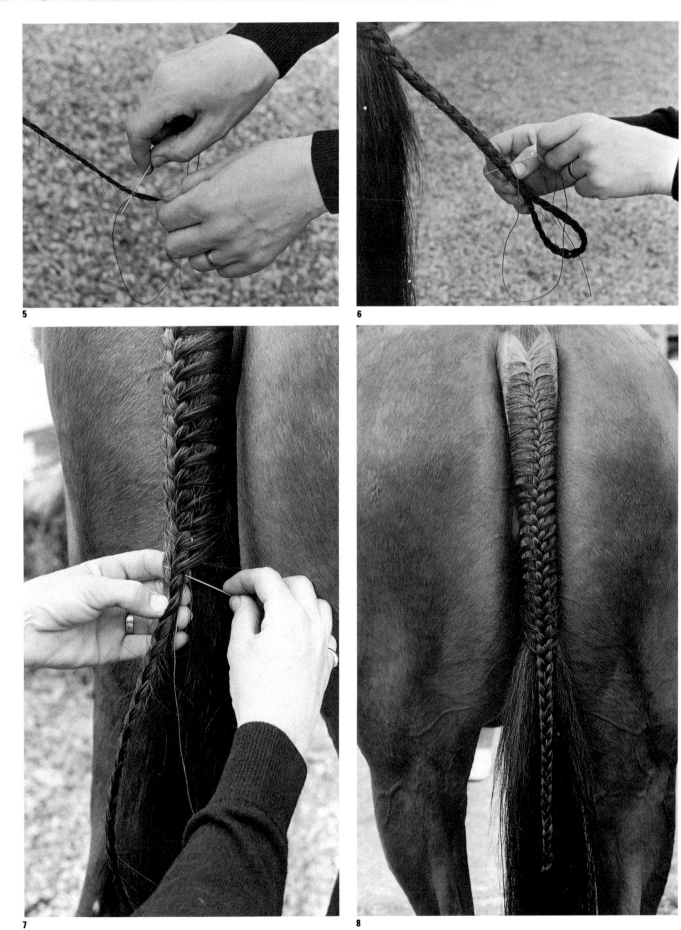

5

6

7

8

# 6
# EXERCISING AND FITNESS

Roadwork and
    Hacking Out  116
Schooling  121
Free Exercise  126

Exercising takes up the major part of the day in most yards, and is vital for the horse's health and for building up condition. All stabled horses should be taken out of their boxes daily, and be given some form of exercise – this may be as schooling, roadwork, hacking, or just a spell of being turned out in the field. A varied exercise plan prevents a horse from going 'sour' and helps him improve in his way of going; the type of work given should be decided according to the different requirements of each horse. For example some horses will benefit from being schooled regularly, others will not; some may not necessarily need to be ridden every day, even over a long while, and a turn out in the paddock suits them best. The work plan will generally depend on the job that the horse is required to do; thus an eventer has to be very fit so a plan of hard work will be necessary to ensure fitness, whereas the show horse need not be subjected to as much work since the level of fitness required is not as great.

In our yard, the tack required for exercising is decided to suit each horse, though basically most will exercise in a snaffle bridle; also the type of noseband used must suit each horse, and be the one he goes best in – a flash noseband or a grakle offers a little more control and stops the horse from opening or crossing his jaw. A standing or a running martingale can also help control a horse, whether in an emergency or if it is just a youngster.

An exercise saddle should be used, usually of a general purpose shape – this is more for the comfort of the rider than the horse. However, it is important to make sure that the saddle fits the horse, and does not rub or pinch it in any way. Most people prefer to use a numnah as it protects the saddle from dirt and grease, and tends to be more comfortable on the horse's back. Whatever the type of numnah and girth that are used, they must be clean to prevent girth galls or sores. Numnahs should be attached properly to the girth straps to prevent them from slipping and scaring the horse, particularly a youngster.

There are many types of boots and bandages that can be used when exercising; generally brushing boots are used in front, and sometimes behind as well, and if working on the road, knee boots should be worn in case the horse slips on the hard surface.

## ROADWORK AND HACKING OUT

Road exercise is an excellent start to a fittening programme as it helps harden up the legs and builds up fitness slowly, without undue strain on wind and muscles. The addition of roadwork and general hacking to a schooling programme prevents boredom and gives a horse a change of scenery, and the chance to get used to strange objects around him. Ridden show horses and ponies also benefit from hacking out on roads and tracks during the season, as this gives them the opportunity to see a variety of different sights and sounds and keeps them fresh in themselves, as well as maintaining fitness and muscle. It is a good idea to work horses on the grass verges where possible, as this will prevent the shoes from wearing down too quickly and will save their legs hammering along on the hard surface. Trotting or cantering on grass will keep them interested and helps them to balance themselves naturally.

The amount of roadwork and hacking that the horse does depends on his job: therefore horses that need a high level of fitness such as eventers or (ordinary) hunters will spend a great deal of time exercising on the road – maybe two hours a day – whilst others will only occasionally ride out; for example the show horse will probably hack out only once or twice a week, just to give him enough variation in his work to keep him happy.

The young horse should always be ridden out in the company of another horse; and if a horse is unsure or unused to riding out along narrow lanes and meeting traffic, an experienced 'schoolmaster' should accompany him. Traffic-shy horses are best kept away from the roads altogether, as car drivers are not always considerate enough to slow down. And if at all possible, never ride along busy main roads as this can be dangerous to yourself, the horse and to drivers.

## LEADING OFF

Being able to ride one horse and lead another is a most convenient solution to exercising more than one horse at a time when perhaps there is a shortage of staff or a large number of horses to take out, or when a novice rider or child must be escorted on a lead rein.

However, it is not an advisable method on major roads, and should really only be carried out by an experienced person with traffic-proof horses. The led horse should wear a bridle with the near-side rein passed through the bit and the animal led close to the lead horse's side, not getting in front or behind; and the led horse should always be held on the side away from the traffic *ie* on the rider's left side.

Conducted incorrectly, this practice could be positively dangerous. Firstly, the equipment used must be safe and sensible. In the photo below, the horses are not equipped safely: first, a leather lead-rein or normal reins should be used, passing through the bit, yet here the rider uses a lunge line which could easily become entangled and is readily dropped. The horses should be wearing brushing boots and knee caps, and the rider's footwear is inadequate. The led horse should always travel with his head at, or just behind the ridden horse's shoulder; and when turning, the led horse should be on the inside with the ridden horse walking around him – if the led horse is dragged around, he will probably not look particularly happy about the manoeuvre!

## HILL WORK

Hill work is an excellent form of exercise, and can help the horse in many ways: it is a good way to improve fitness as it will clear his wind, and will help to develop muscle in all areas of his body but especially in the hindquarters – for some horses, muscle in this area is often insufficiently developed.

Schooling up and down hilly banks can be done on most days, though be sure that the horse is physically fit enough for this sort of work in the first place. Fast work on hills should be kept to a minimum for most show horses – walking and trotting are the most beneficial gaits for toning up muscle and condition. However, as the horse becomes fitter, he will be capable of more hill work.

Lastly, you must always be aware of the type of ground that you will be working on – heavy, muddy going can cause tendon sprains; hard, rutty ground can cause concussion and swelling of the lower limbs.

## JUMPING

It is always important to keep any training programme varied, and jumping is a good way of maintaining the horse's interest in his work. Youngsters especially benefit from popping over small natural hazards such as logs and ditches, and getting used to various objects like this in the course of a hack makes a useful start to their jump training. The horse should wear protective boots to prevent injuries, and a running or standing martingale may be helpful; also use a jumping or general purpose saddle as this enables the rider to keep a better position whilst jumping. There is no reason why any horse – even a show animal that will not be required to jump – should not take on a bit of jumping, as long as it is looked after sensibly; and a young horse should always have the benefit of an experienced rider to help instil confidence.

One of the more usual fences to be encountered in most hunting countries is the natural hedge, and if possible horses should be able to tackle these at home first. Make sure the hedge is free from wire or any other dangerous objects – stakes, bits of metal – and that the place you choose is jumpable – all too often a hedge seems quite alright from one side, yet on the far side there is a large ditch or a steep downhill landing. It is vital that the rider is capable, as horses will often sense any nervousness and consequently lose their own confidence to jump.

After a day's hunting over hedges it is imperative that on return home, the horse's legs are checked thoroughly for thorns, cuts and scrapes; things like this are often missed, but can become quite readily infected and cause considerable swelling and lameness unless treated promptly.

## SCHOOLING

Whether you are interested in competing, or just like riding around the countryside, your horse will give you a better ride if he has had some basic schooling. Regular schooling will help your horse become more balanced and supple, and this will help improve his general way of going and make him a more obedient, comfortable ride.

The basic schooling of any horse, whether it is a hack, cob, riding horse or hunter, should really be the same in the early stages. In fact, the basic work of any competition horse should begin in the same way, the aim being for a well-balanced yet forward-going ride with a good mouth and manners.

Whether you are schooling in an open field or a school, the emphasis must be on suppleness, achieved by frequent changes of pace and some circle work. Hunters and working hunters will need to be fitter and go in a more forward manner. Cobs have a tendency to be strong and lack suppleness so you can never spend too much time working towards improving these aspects. Hacks and riding horses require slightly more training, especially hacks, who need to give an individual show containing changing of legs and a rein back. The hack must also be lighter in the hand to ride and should never pull. Their training, therefore, should be steadier and quieter, concentrating on obedience. Great emphasis should be placed on teaching them to stand still, both on mounting and during a ride.

When introducing a horse to the show-ring, the animal must be accus-

tomed to strange sights and sounds, so taking it to small shows, hunter trials and any equestrian events, even if it does not compete, is sound education. Horses in ridden classes must be used to being ridden by different people so it is a good idea for a friend to ride your horse occasionally. It is advisable for anyone intending to show for the first time to attend one or two of the leading shows as a spectator, to pick up a few hints. There are also various clinics and lectures held on different aspects of showing.

Having said that the basic schooling for any animal is the same, whether it is a hack or a hunter, the sort of ride you would expect in the 'finished product' of the different categories would obviously differ to a certain degree. Thus, the hack must be trained to be as light in the hand as possible: lots of circling and suppling exercises should be included in his schooling, together with work on a loose rein to teach him to carry himself. Work on a loose rein encourages the animal to stretch down lower to the floor and to take a contact from your rein, and is therefore useful in working the top line and strengthening the hind quarters, with the result eventually of making the horse lighter in front. An important point to remember though is that *sufficient impulsion* must still be maintained, even though the reins are loose: this does *not* mean to increase the *speed*, but to maintain the power and energy from behind; this will prevent the hocks from trailing and the horse from tipping on his forehand. The head carriage of the hack should be slightly higher in front, and should never give the rider the feeling of having a downhill ride; the hack should never pull or be strong in your hand. Although the emphasis is on lightness, the head position should also be very still and steady – being light in his mouth because he is fussy and is not accepting his bit, but is backing off it and going behind it, is *not* correct: a fussy mouth which takes no contact at all is quite different from a light, still carriage where the horse maintains an even contact with the rider's hand. It is all these conflicting points that can make the hack so difficult to train, especially as he also needs to have impeccable manners throughout (more than any other show horse), yet must still retain the utmost elegance and be full of presence with his ears pricked and alert.

The riding horse's way of going

should be very similar to that of the hack, but slightly more forward-going, and it can therefore be a little stronger in the hand. A riding horse is required to gallop, so in its whole presentation it should look as if it is in a higher gear; basically it should give the impression of being light and elegant like the hack, but should incline to having the substance of the hunter. Its way of going should therefore be a little more workmanlike.

Hunters must be generally fitter, and so their work programme should include plenty of field work in addition to their basic schooling. The hunter must face his bridle in a bolder manner and take a stronger, more positive contact. However, do not mistake this for a horse that is merely pulling. No horse should pull! He must learn to really cover the ground in the canter, and to lengthen and lower his stride when galloping. Cantering along beside another animal can help to sharpen up a younger or lazier horse, and teach a horse to quicken; but be careful that they don't learn to race each other as you would then be faced with yet another problem when it comes to galloping in the ring with

twenty other competitors. Encouraging a horse to quicken on an uphill gradient – if you are lucky enough to have any hills nearby – is an ideal way to get him to lengthen his stride and lower his head; it is obviously the ideal way to increase general fitness as well.

The increase and decrease of pace to and from gallop is equally important: the horse must still be very well balanced, as nothing looks worse than a rider trying to pull up from the gallop in the ring with the horse's head on the floor, having had to take another complete circuit in order to do so. The horse must learn to be immediately responsive to your aids, and to pull up in a balanced manner. Plenty of work in lengthening and shortening your pace at the canter is an invaluable exercise, and can be done in the field, in a school or even on the grass verge.

Cobs should be trained using a combination of the methods for the hack and the hunter. They must be mannerly and fairly steady in their general paces, but must be able to quicken and gallop like a hunter. The main criticism of cobs is that they can be strong and heavy, giving a very wooden ride which is most undesirable. Steady suppling work is invaluable, making them bend around your inside leg on the corners, and plenty of upward and downward transitions and changes of pace will help lighten the forehand.

It is worth experimenting with bits for the cob – or for any horse, for that matter. You may be lucky enough to have an animal with a good mouth that will be suited to the first double bridle you try him in; with others you may not be so lucky and you may have to change tactics several times. Most cobs will accept a double bridle, and usually a fairly long curb bit; most will also accept a chain-type curb chain, whereas your hack may go more kindly in an elastic or leather one. A lot of cobs go well in a pelham bit, that gives a little more leverage and control. Finding the right bit can play an important part in the producing of a cob, which must be able to gallop on, yet still pull up in a well balanced, mannerly fashion like the hunter. Likewise when ridden by the judge he must not give the feeling that he is leaning heavily towards the floor and try to run away. The ride a cob gives the judge is often his downfall, and often the reason for an apparently smart-looking animal being demoted a few places.

## DRAW-REINS

There are many gadgets and artificial aids available, that claim to assist the schooling process; draw-reins are just one and are effective *if used correctly* – and a rider should really only use draw-reins if he or she is experienced enough to understand their effect. Remember that the horse is not necessarily working properly simply because his head is lowered and tucked in. The hindquarters should always come right underneath the horse in work, but if the rider uses insufficient leg, they will not, and the horse will fall on his forehand; he will then find it almost impossible to move in a balanced and organised way. Thus draw-reins should not make a horse go in a tense, rigid outline: they should simply encourage it to work with a lower head carriage and a rounder outline. They also help the rider to gain more control of the horse, especially the headstrong type. Draw-reins should not be used on your horse every day, but only when necessary; otherwise he will quite likely learn to lean on them, and this will bring him onto the forehand and make him heavy in the rider's hand – which rather defeats the object.

## THE SCHOOLING AREA

It is quite possible to school in various places – in a field or paddock, on a headland – but having a purpose-made school is definitely a great advantage. An all-weather surface such as the one illustrated can be used throughout the year and avoids any worries about seasonal ground conditions; thus not only does it help to have a school like this when the ground gets muddy and wet in winter, it is also invaluable should it become dry and very hard in the summer – in both circumstances it saves the horses' legs from being jarred or strained on a bad surface. This type of school can be used for a variety of work: jumping, dressage, long-reining and lungeing.

As long as the correct materials are used right from the beginning, the amount of care and maintenance will be kept to a minimum; though ultimately, how successful the surface proves to be depends on the foundations and the drainage. The most common all-weather surfaces include woodchips, sand, rubber and PVC. Woodchips are suitable for all purposes, and drain easily; some sand is not suitable and tends to freeze; rubber

is hard-wearing and quite successful – it provides a good surface and requires little upkeep, though it tends to smell in hot weather.

The size of an outdoor school depends on individual budget, but basically the bigger it is, the better. Horses do not benefit from schooling in small, tight areas and this practice can be positively harmful to their limbs.

General maintenance work would include ensuring that the fencing is safe, and levelling off the surface regularly to prevent certain areas becoming deep. Occasionally the surface may become thin when it should be given an extra topping; an inadequate surface covering could create more serious problems in the event of the lining beneath becoming ripped. Otherwise there is little else to consider; a sand or woodchip surface may need watering in very dry weather, to lay the dust.

The main disadvantage of having an outdoor surface rather than an indoor school is that extreme weather conditions such as heavy rain, snow or frost will inevitably restrict its use; but then the difference in the cost of construction is great. The cost of building an outdoor arena varies according to the type of surface that is required and also the area that is to be used; for example if the land is steep, a great deal of preparation will be necessary so as to achieve a level surface, thereby increasing labour costs considerably.

The indoor school is a luxury to most yards, and normally the cost proves to be too high. Basically the area necessary is much the same, although the foundations will involve more work to provide for concreting the uprights. The main complication concerning any indoor arena is that planning permission is required.

The photograph shows an indoor school of exceptional quality. It is large, approximately 88 by 44yd (80 x 40m), and the gallery area provides seating for a hundred people for lecture demonstration purposes. The surface is a PVC type which is quite light, and does not become deep like some sand can.

A well-constructed school will have as much natural light coming through the roof as possible. An important part of maintaining an indoor school is to prevent it from becoming dusty; this requires regular watering, for which an overhead waterer system is excellent.

The cost of this type of school is very high, however, and not many establishments can justify the cost.

## FREE EXERCISE

All horses benefit from being turned out in the field as a form of exercise, and for the stabled horse it is very important that he is allowed time to 'play', without being greatly restricted. Going out in the field gives horses a sense of freedom in their natural environment, somewhere they can indulge any high spirits and have a roll. A good routine for competition horses, and one they will thrive on, allows for them to go out every day; in fact some horses become difficult, and hard to control and handle if they are kept in all the time and exercised for only a short while, so a spell in the field will be very beneficial.

Late spring and summer is a time when horses appreciate going out — though having said that, it is important not to leave your competition horse out when he is standing by the gate waiting to come in because he is cold, or wet, or the flies are bad. Equally it may be better not to turn him out in winter when the ground is very muddy and there is nothing for him to graze; he will only get himself into trouble or develop skin infections such as mud fever, cracked heels, or rain scald. If your horse is valuable or prone to injuring himself when he is turned out, he should wear protective boots – brushing boots and over-reach boots. In cold weather provide him with a New Zealand rug, and let him keep a good coat. If there is a restriction to the field, grazing in hand can often be beneficial.

# 7
# VETERINARY CARE AND SHOEING

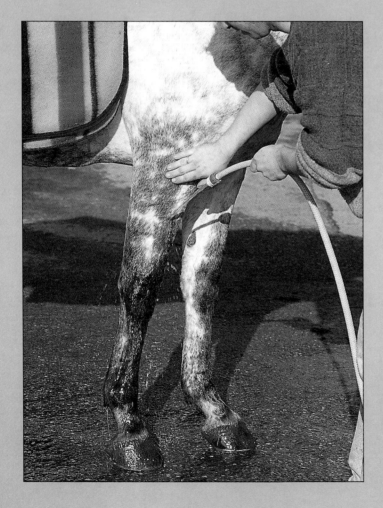

**Basic Health
Checks 128
Recognising
Lameness 131
Leg Injuries 132
Rubbing 133
Shoeing and Foot
Care 134**

## BASIC HEALTH CHECKS

Recognising when a horse is unhealthy is a very important part of stable management: make a point of noticing its general appearance, the state of its droppings, how well it looks in its coat, whether it has eaten up normally. The state of the bedding often provides a good clue as to a horse's well-being: a dug-up bed or straw in random heaps usually indicates a problem such as colic or a virus. Viruses these days come in many different forms and can be very severe; if undetected in the early stages, untold and irreparable damage can be done to the horse's health if it is worked and not treated.

Here are some points to look out for: if a horse has not eaten up; swelling of the hind legs; discharge from the eyes or nostrils; a horse appearing to blow for no reason; or which, out of the stable, appears lifeless, sweats up unduly, or appears to be tired even when fit. Any of these signs indicate ill-health, and may call for a veterinary visit. Never transport horses that are unwell, as travelling can be very stressful, particularly over long distances.

Colic in the horse is similar to the human stomach ache, and is any form of abdominal pain. Over the years there have been different schools of thought in how best to deal with it. However, if the colic is severe, you must prevent the horse from rolling, although it may not be necessary to walk it. Generally, if colic symptoms of kicking and wanting to roll do not subside after twenty minutes, a vet should be called. If the symptoms have gone the horse can then be allowed to munch on hay or bran mash at will.

Colic cannot always be avoided, no matter how much care or attention is given. Problems can, however, be caused by feeding; for example, new forage or too large quantities. Horses turned out very occasionally may tend to gorge excessively if grass is available, so it may be best to introduce grass slowly, by allowing perhaps half an hour at a time until the horse becomes more accustomed to it. Some horses are prone to colic if they are suffering from stress, such as excessive travelling, so always check a horse once it has reached its destination.

Regular use of Epsom salts in the diet is believed to help prevent the onset of colic and related disorders.

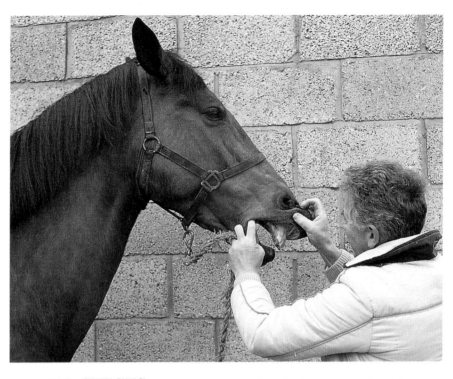

### DENTAL CHECKS

Dental checks should be as much part of health management as regular shoeing. Unfortunately problems within the horse's mouth are often neglected.

A horse with a painful mouth will not be able to concentrate and work properly. He will do his best to evade pain, thus causing an unsteadiness in the hand, and fighting and pulling against any contact with the bit. Sharp edges in the teeth can cut the inside of the cheeks, as well as causing rubbing on the tongue. It is best to carry out a regular check-up approximately every six months.

### EYE INSPECTION

A part of any veterinary examination is an inspection of the eyes. This is done in two parts: first, the outside of the eye is checked for abnormalities such as tumours or other growths, injured eyelids, any discharge or infections, lumps or any other injuries; it is then inspected using an ophthalmoscope, which can reveal conditions otherwise undetectable.

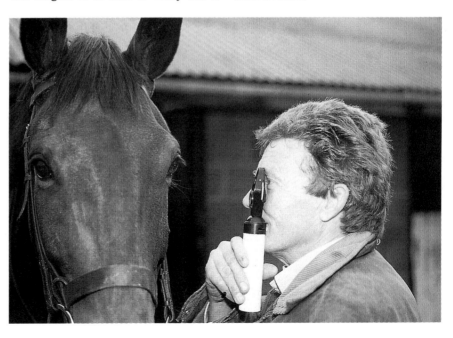

## PULSE

To take a horse's pulse use the facial artery which passes under the jaw, or the Median artery in the centre of the inside of the foreleg, level with the elbow; the fingers should be placed under the pulse point. When the horse is at rest, the correct pulse rate should be between 36 to 42 beats per minute; it will be considerably elevated following stress, up to 60 beats per minute during fast strenuous work, but this should return to normal within 10 to 15 minutes if the horse is rested (providing he is sufficiently fit for the work carried out). It is a good idea to know your own horse's normal pulse rate and usual recovery rate because these can vary a great deal from one horse to another.

The normality of a horse's heart has always been of major concern to vets and horse owners – the heart is obviously highly important in athletic performance, and any defect is considered likely to impose limits to the horse's achievement.

The veterinary surgeon is checking the horse's heart rate in the photograph below; this is carried out as a matter of procedure during a veterinary examination.

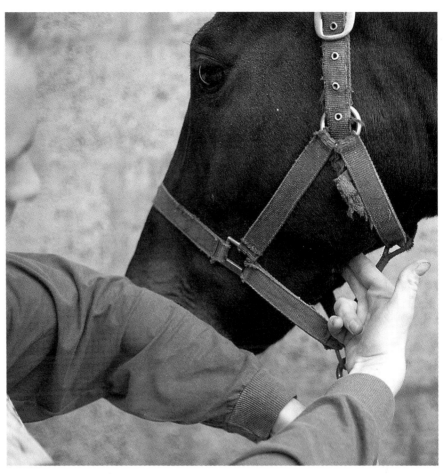

## TEMPERATURE

Taking the horse's temperature is a good way of assessing its general health. A proper large animal thermometer should be used; a digital type is excellent to gain an accurate reading.

Place it in the horse's rectum, holding it firmly so that it cannot be drawn in should the muscles contract; after 60 seconds it should be removed and read. The normal temperature of an adult horse is 100°–100.5° F (38°C); in a foal it is from 100°F to 101.5°F. A rise over 102°F is abnormal, and a temperature of 104° to 105°F is serious, and a veterinary surgeon should be called.

## RESPIRATION

To check the respiration rate stand behind the horse and watch its flanks,

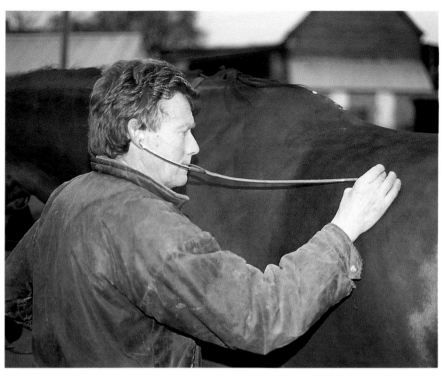

and count the number of times that they rise and fall in one minute – each rise and fall is counted as one breath. The breathing should be even, at the rate of eight to fifteen breaths per minute when the horse is at rest; he should be able to breathe easily, and should make no noises whilst doing so.

In the photograph above the veterinary surgeon is listening for any abnormalities in the working of the lungs.

## VACCINATIONS

Vaccination against tetanus and equine influenza is a very important part of any stable management routine. Each horse should have its own vaccination card, and it is the owner or groom's responsibility that this is kept up to date by a veterinary surgeon, whose advice should be taken as to when, and how often booster injections need to be given. Some large shows, sales and studs will not admit a horse which cannot be shown to possess an up-to-date certificate. The site of injection will be up to the individual veterinary surgeon, in the chest, neck or rump.

## WORMING

All horses should be wormed every six to eight weeks, whether at grass or stabled. To prevent a horse's system building up an immunity, the brand and wormer type should be changed periodically; and it is important always to worm new arrivals before turning them out to pasture. Worm-infested horses will look poor in condition and generally lack-lustre, in which case veterinary advice should be sought. Once administered the containers should be disposed of carefully and not left lying around.

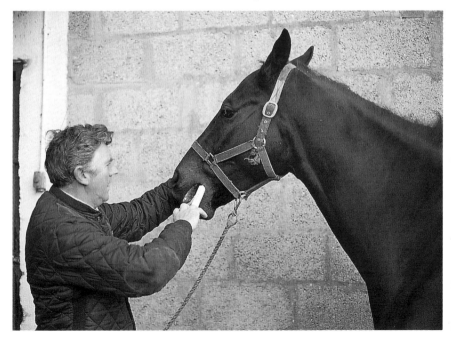

## RECOGNISING LAMENESS

One of the most important aspects of stable management is being able to recognise and diagnose lameness. In the stabled horse, lameness is often acute; look for heat and swelling, and if none is apparent and the lameness seems to have appeared 'out of nowhere', then there are several conditions to which it might be attributed: it could be the onset of laminitis, in which case the horse is likely to be sitting back on its haunches; if it is resting one particular leg this may indicate a poisoned foot, or injury from a blacksmith's nail ('nail-bind'); or perhaps the animal has been cast during the night. It is important to find out or establish which limb is affected. Lead the horse out of its box if possible, and how it moves will give you a better guide as to the cause of the lameness. It is the horse which is only very slightly lame, or *just* unlevel, or only lame on the turn which is the hardest to diagnose. With no obvious swelling of the limbs it is often prudent to call in the farrier first of all and have the shoe removed; and if after the farrier's investigation there is still no recognisable or apparent cause, then do not fail to call the veterinary surgeon immediately.

Trotting up a horse in hand when investigating lameness must be carried out correctly to give the observer the best possible chance of identifying the nature of the lameness. The surface used should be flat and hard, and the assistant leading should always trot the horse up on a slack rein. Turning the horse on a tight circle, in both directions, will often show up a lameness problem in a foreleg, though less so in a hind. The seat of severe lameness is probably low down, in the foot, otherwise much higher up in the shoulder, though the latter is less common.

When nursing a sick horse in conjunction with veterinary instructions there are certain things that should always be done: the horse should be protected from chills – lightweight blankets should be used, and a clean deep bed provided; it should be given a more laxative diet in small, easy-to-eat feeds; and finally temperature, pulse and respiration should be taken regularly and recorded, noting any variation from the normal.

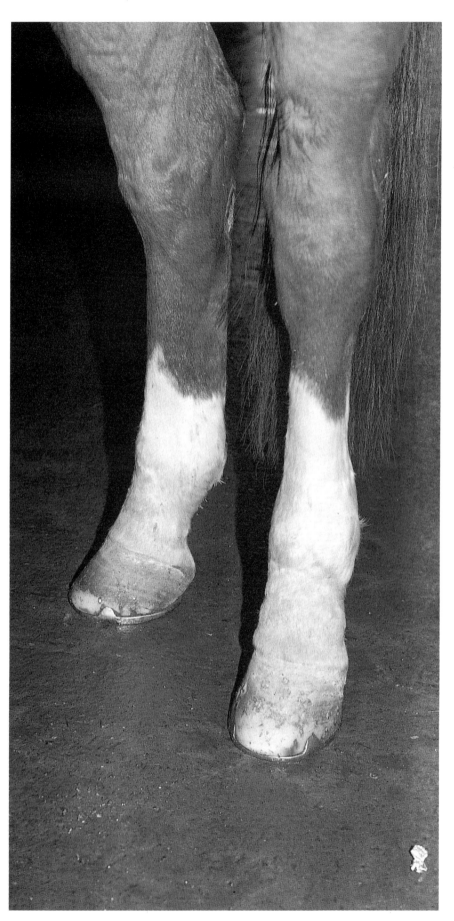

# LEG INJURIES

### SWOLLEN LIMBS

Swollen hind legs are very often a tell-tale sign of a horse not in the best of health. This may have a variety of causes: over-feeding and under-work; over-work on hard ground; a change in the diet, and in particular feeding a new season's hay to stabled horses; virus infection; and more usually in winter conditions, mud fever and cracked heels – all these can cause the legs to inflame. It is important to detect any obvious cause, if possible, and treat accordingly. Bandaging will help to reduce swelling, as will letting stabled horses out in the paddock, or a programme of light exercise; it is usually helpful to feed a basic diet of bran mash with a handful of Epsom salts. Failure to identify the cause of swollen limbs and administer treatment can lead to legs of the most horrendous size.

### BIG KNEE

A big knee (opposite above left) is usually the result of external influence, injury caused by falling over on the road, a kick from another horse, hitting a fence whilst jumping, even banging at the stable door. Treatment would entail initially cold hosing, followed by poulticing at night. The Wurlyboot is a useful item to have for any knee injury that requires cold water hosing. The boot is fastened on and a hose attached to it so that the horse can be left tied up while the knee is being treated, so avoiding the need to hold a hose for ten to twenty minutes each time.

When bandaging a knee it is advisable to use cotton wool and gamgee, particularly behind the knee, in order to prevent further injury to this area; a leg bandage applied first will help to prevent the knee bandage slipping down the leg. Treatment by ultrasonic machine will also help to bring down any swelling, though this must be administered by an experienced person or under veterinary supervision.

As the knee reduces in size it is important not to stop treatment too soon because the filling may all too quickly re-appear. The horse will almost certainly benefit from walking exercise during the treatment.

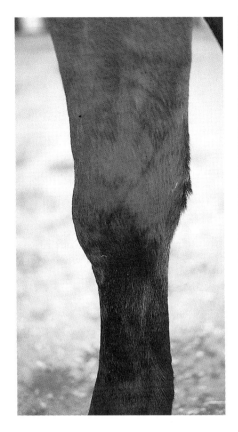

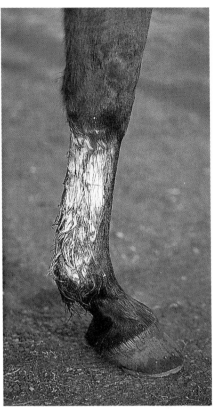

## INJURIES

An external leg injury can vary from a simple cut to a major laceration, but whatever the size or severity, remember that any open wound or abrasion can readily become infected if it is not treated properly. With minor wounds the whole area should be cleaned, and an antiseptic spray or cream applied to the injury; anything more serious should not be left simply to heal itself but the vet called to advise.

Similarly there are varying degrees of strain or sprain to tendons and ligaments, and some horses are more prone to this sort of injury than others; it is often caused by working in wet, muddy, heavy ground conditions. The vet should always be called if this sort of leg injury is suspected, and will advise specific treatment; generally box-rest is required. However, there are numerous leg pastes and plasters on the market that can be used to alleviate swelling and promote correct healing in cases of minor strain. The photograph shows kaolin paste applied in the treatment of a foreleg injury.

## RUBBING

Normally rug rubs occur on the shoulder, usually when the rug constantly slips backwards. The bare patch on the chest as shown in the picture is not as common; however, this can occur if the rug is a very bad fit. Adding a second rug of a soft material, or a blanket, to lie against the horse's skin will help to prevent such problems. It is, however, important that each horse has properly fitting clothing.

Make sure the length, depth and shape are correct: length is measured from the point of the withers to the edge of the rug by the tail. The rug should come to the base of the neck (and *not* lie back over the withers). Most of the newer rugs are now shaped to fit the horse's topline, with darts at shoulder, stifle and rear to fit the body shape: this design, together with cross-surcingles, completely eliminates the problem of the rug slipping. Be sure that the shaping over the quarters is in the correct place, otherwise the whole rug will tend to slip back and put pressure on the withers; also that the horse has enough room over the point of the shoulder (from withers to centre-front buckle) – a horse with a big front and a sloping shoulder may need a larger size rug than his length would indicate.

The main problems experienced with rugs and rollers are caused by pressure, by rubbing or slipping. Some horses seem particularly susceptible to chafing even when their rugs fit well, usually on the point of shoulder, withers, back and sometimes hip bones. On the back, where the roller goes, sew in a fleecy padding; or wither pads, with a channel made by cutting into foam rubber; or two soft pads fixed to the roller on either side of the spine. Rubbing on the shoulder can be prevented by sewing a patch/strip of satin skirt material, or tough shiny plastic, to the inside of the rug, big enough to cover the rubbed area adequately. Also available now are hoods-cum-shoulder covers made of 'neuropen': these are pulled over the horse's head into place, and prevent chafing of the shoulders and withers.

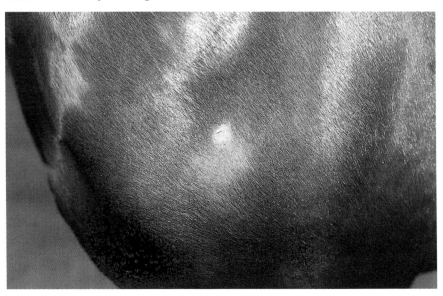

## SHOEING AND FOOT CARE

The old saying 'No foot, no horse' is taken very seriously by anyone who has anything to do with horses. Neglect of the feet of any horse or pony indicates very poor stable management. It is amazing the number of animals that still have scant attention paid to the feet, and the riders who continue to ride with the horse's shoes hanging off, in total disregard of their own and their horse's safety. Furthermore, many people persist in breeding animals with poor foot conformation, and continue to leave the feet of their youngstock in a bad state. An animal's welfare is at stake if his feet are neglected, and only irregular attention can result in injury, disease, foot infections and lameness. It is vital that your horse is correctly shod and his feet kept in good condition: if you can take the trouble to learn as much as possible about the actual structure of a horse's foot you will be better able to appreciate the skill that is required by the farrier.

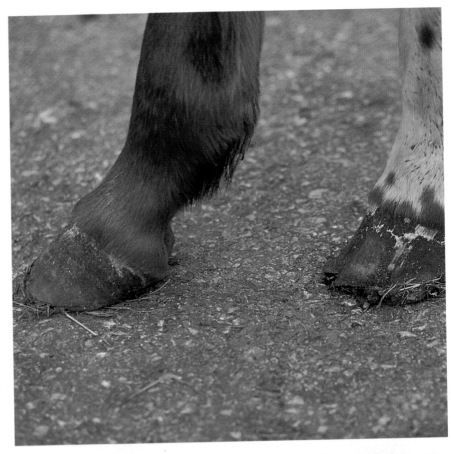

Compare the overgrown, neglected feet of the animal in the first photograph with those of the second which shows a well-shod, well-balanced foot; the shoe is neither too heavy nor too light, the nails are level and approximately a third of the height of the hoof. The whole thing looks neat and tidy.

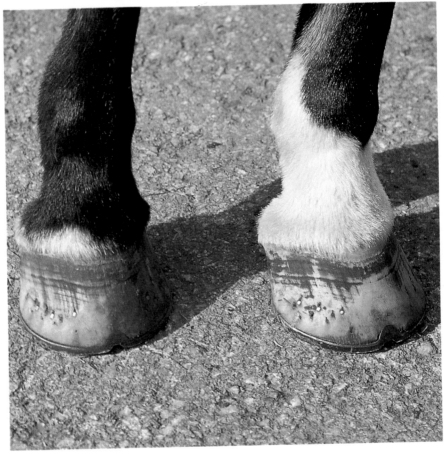

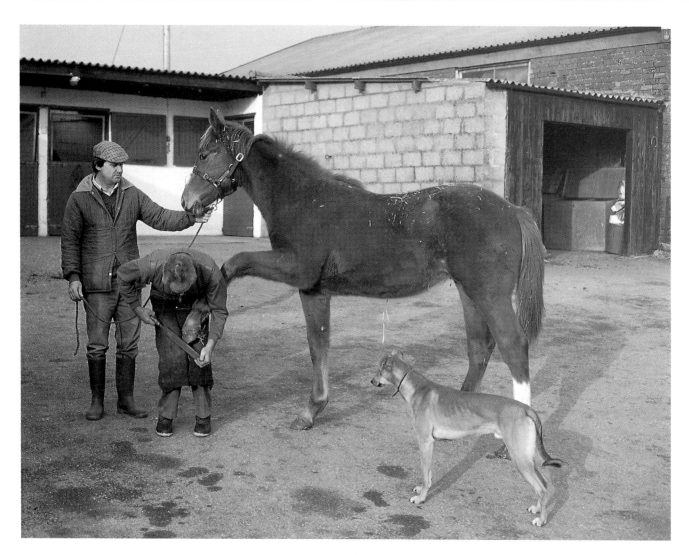

On average, horses will need shoeing every month, though if they are doing a lot of work on the road the farrier's visit could be more often. On the other hand, if they spend most of their time in the field, the shoes will last longer – *but* even so they will probably need a refit every six weeks. Nor should unshod horses at grass be forgotten: they should have their feet trimmed at least every six to eight weeks, otherwise the hoof will grow too long, then crack and break up.

It is essential to have a good relationship with your farrier – for example, do not expect him to catch the horse out of the field himself, and do not bring it in all covered in mud to be shod. Do not expect him to be able to shoe any horse correctly in deep-litter bedding, or in any other unsuitable place. If you think your horse has a specific problem that could benefit from remedial shoeing, ask him to watch it trotted up in hand so he can see how it moves – there is probably something he can do to help

or improve it. Unfortunately all too often there is disagreement between the farrier, horse owner and sometimes the veterinary surgeon and tempers are lost; but if commonsense is allowed to prevail then a satisfactory solution can usually be resolved as to how the horse should be shod, in its own best interests.

---

## MAKING A BRAN POULTICE

To make a bran poultice mix one to two scoops of dry bran in a bucket or pan and pour on enough boiling water to wet the bran thoroughly. When cool enough to immerse your hand, put the contents into a foot poultice boot and strap this to the foot. Alternatively, pour the mixture into a sack or bag and bandage to the foot. Leave the poultice for twelve hours.

---

It is important that care of the feet is a regular occurrence from foalhood onwards; this practice also accustoms youngstock to the farrier. There should always be someone to hold a young horse – this seems to give it more confidence, and avoids unnecessary accidents. Leaving the feet untrimmed leads to cracks and splits in the hoof, and causes undue wear on the joints; moreover any abnormality in the horse's conformation will be greatly exacerbated if the feet are left untrimmed. Many faults can be put right, to a greater or lesser degree, if they are worked on at an early age, and much can be done by a good farrier who would hope to improve the shape of a hoof and maybe the straightness of a leg, by regular trimming.

This yearling is having its feet rasped. Although this youngster is standing quietly, an open yard is not the ideal place for the farrier to attend to it: it would be better and safer in a stable.

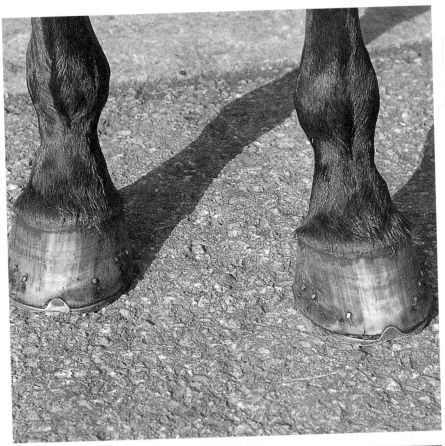

## DAILY MAINTENANCE

The shod horse in work should be inspected regularly to see if it needs re-shoeing. Risen nail clenches, as shown here, indicate that a refit or new shoes will soon be required, and it is important to notice if they have because in that case they must be knocked down with a hammer before exercise to prevent them cutting into the inside of the opposite leg. If worn shoes are neglected they can easily come off, causing injury or a badly broken-up foot. It is a false economy for a horse in regular work not to be shod every four to five weeks. A good example of a horse in need of new shoes can be seen in the photograph below left; the outer edge of the shoe is worn flat and uneven, and the toe is considerably worn.

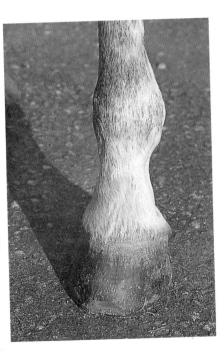

Horses that do a lot of roadwork or are ridden and led, often drag a hind toe and wear it off square (see above photograph), either through laziness or because they are ridden badly. Some farriers will recommend a rolled toe shoe, or have heavier iron welded into the hind shoe. For the ordinary riding horse which has this habit it is preferable to ride on grass as much as possible. Often owners ask to have heavy shoes put on in the hope of them lasting longer, but this does not always follow. Always take the farrier's advice on this matter.

Sometimes a horse or pony will object to having its feet attended to. This may just be nervousness, in which case great patience should be shown, and every effort made to reassure it. On the rare occasion an animal is really difficult it may be necessary to use a twitch in order to gain greater control and thus lessen the risk of injury to either farrier or horse. This may be a 'humane' twitch, made of two solid metal pieces hinged together and which will exert only a certain degree of pressure; or the traditional twitch which consists of a wooden handle and rope and which can be twisted very tightly indeed.

If you live near a farrier's forge and have only a few horses, it may be more convenient if you take them there for

shoeing, as the farrier will have everything that he should need to hand. Having said that, this practice is now unfortunately becoming a thing of the past, superseded by the modern travelling forge fully furnished with up-to-date equipment. Many travelling farriers shoe cold, nowadays, with ready-made and measured shoes; the main difference seems to be in the actual fitting of the shoe which is possibly better done hot. Horses that are not used to the smoke caused when shoeing hot will need to be carefully introduced and held by an assistant for a time or two.

The cost of new shoes depends on the area, but varies between £30 and £45, plus farrier's travelling expenses and any studs and stud-holes.

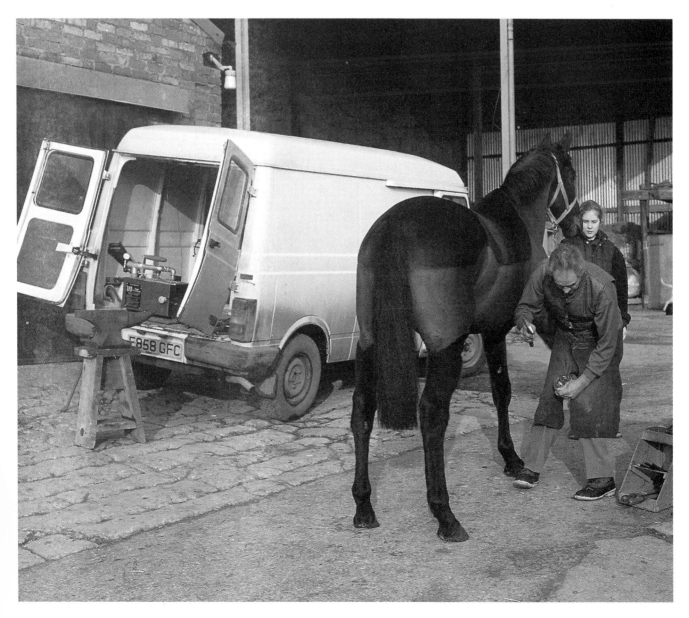

## TYPES OF SHOE

Nowadays there are different types of shoe available to suit the different equestrian purpose, including some that are now fixed without nails – these use a strong glue, though as yet they have not found much favour. The farrier can also fit the horse's shoes either with driven road studs, or stud-holes which will take screw-in studs; there is a variety of studs for use in competition depending on the job the horse has to do, and in what type of ground it is working.

Normally studs are only fitted in the hind shoes, though in some cases they are fitted in front as well. Stud-holes are made by the farrier when he makes the shoes, and either threaded to take screw-in studs, or driven, when a road stud is tapped in before the shoe is fitted.

Note that a horse should not be ridden on tarmac wearing competition studs as damage can be caused to the limbs as well as the hoof because of its bodyweight bearing unevenly on the hoof surface.

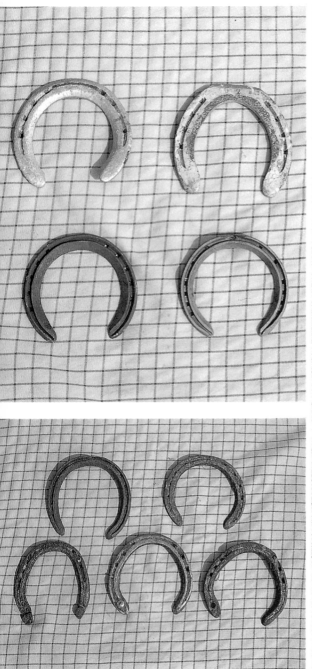

# 8
# TRANSPORT

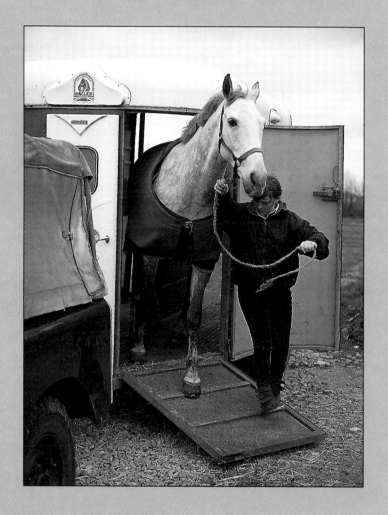

**Horsebox and Trailer Design  140**
**Dressing the Horse for Travel  142**
**Loading  143**
**Unloading  145**
**Transport Overseas  147**
**International Travel  147**

Nowadays transporting horses and ponies is an everyday affair, and long distances are travelled to many equestrian events. This may be in a one-horse trailer towed behind the family car, or in the luxury £100,000 lorry – the choice is so wide, and when buying, the different options must be considered very seriously so that the needs of the individual person are best suited. For example, a trailer is probably more useful for the small stable yard and for the person with just one or two horses or ponies, whereas the big jumping or showing yard would need a lorry that could take four or even six horses, with live-in accommodation, and the engine power to cover many miles as quickly and safely as possible.

Good driving is vital, whether the transport is a lorry or a towing vehicle and trailer – many a horse has been turned into a bad traveller or become unwilling to load because of fast, bad driving. A driver with little or no experience of driving horses would be advised to make several trips without a horse on board, and in particular to practise reversing and turning. In the event of having to borrow transport, be quite sure that everything is in order, and that not only is the driver qualified, but properly insured too and with experience of driving horses. It is also a wise precaution always to have someone with the driver, particularly when transporting youngstock – though never let anybody travel in the trailer itself, as this is illegal.

Some horses will travel perfectly well in a lorry but not in a trailer, even to the point of coming down; sometimes, however, removing the partition in a trailer will help the animal balance and so travel more comfortably. It is also advisable to have some form of bedding, even on a rubber-floored vehicle, not only to help prevent slipping but to make cleaning out easier; this also encourages animals to stale if they so wish – many horses will not relieve themselves onto a bare floor.

At the start of any journey, be careful to travel slowly and steadily to give the animals a chance to settle down; once they are settled and if all is well, speed can be increased. And even before starting out, it is essential to check oil and water levels and also tyre pressures, also that enough fuel is in the tank to get you to your destination. A full medical box plus a spare headcollar and rope should always be taken on each journey. On long journeys it is advisable to stop every hour or two and check that everything is in order – a very much easier task, of course, in lorries which have a walk-through area purpose-built for inspecting the horses or ponies.

Whether you have a lorry or a trailer, all vehicles benefit from regular maintenance: they should be washed with a hose or jet washer regularly to remove dirt from the paintwork, thus minimising the risk of rust; and they should also be regularly serviced, and any minor repairs done immediately. One disadvantage of owning a lorry rather than a trailer is the expense first of buying, then keeping another vehicle on the road – a costly business when you consider tax, insurance, servicing and general repairs. Many trailer owners use the tow vehicle as the everyday car, thus avoiding the expense of having a second vehicle.

# HORSEBOX AND TRAILER DESIGN

## TRAILERS

The range of trailers currently available on the market is vast, and the choice regarding size, style, colour and so on is enormous: at one end of the scale is the inexpensive single trailer, at the other the luxury three-horse model with 'live-in' area similar to that of a purpose-built lorry; this area normally includes tack space and day-living facilities such as a sink and hob. It is even possible now to buy a trailer which takes four horses. A hose fitment for washing down is included in some of the newer models. Modern materials and styling have cut down on maintenance, but do not neglect to keep regular checks on the trailer, particularly the flooring, brakes and lights. These should be service-checked at least every six months, and checked over for damage every time the trailer is used.

The purchase of a secondhand trailer needs serious consideration: be sure to check that both floor and ramp are

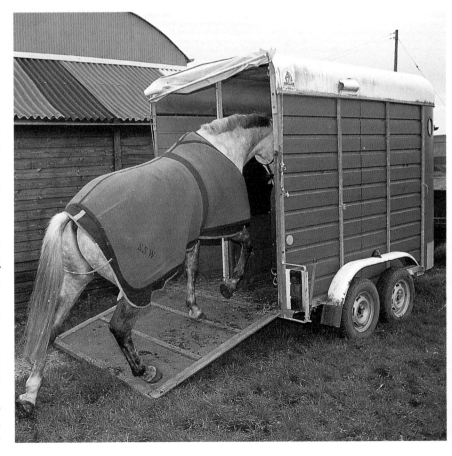

sound, also tyres, of course including the spare wheel. It is also wise to ask an experienced person to inspect it prior to purchase. Alternatively you could always go to a reputable dealer, an option which equally applies when purchasing a lorry. However, it is better to have a good sound trailer with a tow vehicle, than an old, unreliable lorry. If you have the choice when purchasing a trailer, opt for a front-unload model: it is much easier for loading and unloading, and at a show the top door above the front ramp can be left open so the horse can look out.

Never use a trailer which is too small for your horse: many even of the more modern designs are too small to accommodate two full-size 16.2hh horses, so take care that you select a model big enough for your requirements.

Be sure to hitch up the trailer correctly to the towing vehicle, and that the hitch is the right height; use a safety wire at all times.

## HORSEBOXES

The two-horse aluminium horsebox, ideal for the competitive amateur and in particular for the lady driver, is easy to drive and does not require an HGV licence. It has a low-loading side ramp, is easily maintained and serviced, and requires minimum parking space – a distinct advantage when going hunting, especially if you need to park at the meet.

For the large sponsored competition yard or the millionaire owner, the choice in the luxury horsebox market is unlimited. The facilities can be palatial, to say the least – up to six horses comfortably partitioned, and human accommodation second to none. Nevertheless, these boxes do need great care as regards maintenance and in their everyday use; also drivers must hold an HGV licence. Many of these more wealthy yards have their own driver, and both the lorry and the transportation of the horses are entirely his responsibility.

Unfortunately, these vehicles lose their value rapidly, even after only a few years, since even when they become old and cheap, they are still not suitable for the average horse owner; whereas the smaller, more practical lorry is far more likely to hold its value.

# DRESSING THE HORSE FOR TRAVEL

Most people take the precaution of dressing their horses in protective clothing before a journey; legs are the most vulnerable, so you might find, in the horse's wardrobe, a set of travelling bandages; a pair of knee caps, the top strap comfortably tight when worn and the lower strap loose; a pair of hock boots, of which there are many now on the market; and also many varieties of travelling boots – though personally I always feel greater support is given to the legs and the joints with bandages.

A nylon or leather headcollar should be worn – many feel leather is safer as it will break in an emergency; and prefer it to a nylon headcollar which is essentially unbreakable.

What clothing the horse should wear depends entirely on the time of year, the fitness of the animal, and the distance to be travelled – some horses like just a sheet, and others will be more comfortable in a woollen day-rug. When long distances are travelled, it may be necessary to change the cloth-

ing en route, according to the climate prevailing. Many professional horse transporters have well-partitioned, padded lorries, and prefer the horse not to have boots or bandages on its legs in case these become untied or slip right down around its feet. Be careful not to put tail bandages on too tight when travelling, as this may result in the loss of hair if the bandages are left on during a long journey; a tail guard without a bandage is probably safest.

# LOADING

One of the first essentials when loading a horse or pony is to stay calm and self-possessed, especially with young or nervous animals. Make sure you are positioned on a good, level, non-slippery surface; approach the ramp squarely and purposefully, do not walk ahead and face the horse, and never try to *pull* it into a box or trailer; with awkward loaders or young horses it may be helpful to park the vehicle alongside a wall or building, or back it up to the stable door if possible, in order to gain greater control of the animal. Straw can be laid down on the ramp to give a horse more confidence, or a loading ramp if available can be used.

Lead the horse quietly to the edge of the ramp, and hopefully he will walk in sensibly. It is always advisable, even with an older horse, to put a snaffle bridle over the headcollar for extra control – many horses will try to swing aside and run off when being loaded, and with any young or difficult animal it is essential that it has a bit in its mouth. A bucket with feed in will sometimes help, as will getting an assistant to place one or both of the animal's forelegs on the bottom of the ramp to help it gain confidence. However, beware that it doesn't suddenly rush in, or that having gone in, it doesn't immediately run straight backwards – this habit can be particularly dangerous when loading into a trailer. With a trailer, always make sure the safety back-strap is fastened before attempting to put the back ramp up.

Horses should be taught to load and unload several times at home before any journey is attempted so that the whole operation becomes second nature to them; away from home in a strange place they will invariably refuse to load unless they have been properly taught.

Once loaded, make sure the horse is tied up comfortably, not so short that he cannot hold his head normally, nor too long so he risks getting tangled in the lead-rope. Horses which chew ropes should have a rack chain – but never, under any circumstances and however quiet the animal, tie a horse up with a chain, as the risk of it catching a hand or fingers is high.

## THE DIFFICULT LOADER

The horse or pony that is difficult to load is an abomination – though having said that, patience and care should always be demonstrated with young or nervous horses, and everything done to help them, from straw on the ramp to a bucket of feed. Using a lunge line is often a great help, though be careful the animal does not kick back – sometimes this method works wonders, at other times it does not. In the case of the difficult, naughty older horse that is just being troublesome, experienced help should be sought – though sometimes just a good smack with a lunge whip will make him pay attention, renew his respect and persuade him to walk in. Following another horse or pony will often persuade a horse to load.

Foals or yearlings, and sometimes even ponies can be helped to load by two people linking hands behind their haunches and half lifting them in; but be careful not to get kicked. Difficult animals often throw their heads up to avoid entering the lorry or trailer; these can be fitted with a tight standing martingale buckled to a surcingle, which should prevent them throwingup their head and getting out of control.

Whatever happens when loading any animal, it should be impressed upon all helpers how vital it is to keep calm, as any loss of temper or outburst of impatience could result in the whole operation becoming really fraught and potentially disastrous.

Some horses will travel quietly, but others will not, and for the latter it sometimes helps to move the partition over to give lesser or greater space. Beware of the horse that attempts to lie down – this sort is a danger to himself and to others, and is often better travelled alone for a time or two until it gains confidence.

## UNLOADING

Be careful when unloading that the animal does not attempt to jump from the top of the ramp; allow it plenty of time to come down slowly, and *never* chase it out as there is always the danger of it slipping or falling down. As much care needs to be taken when unloading as it does when loading – in particular this applies to trailers. If possible, try to avoid making horses back out: hence the advantage of a front ramp.

## TRAVELLING HORSES TOGETHER

Obviously it is advisable to protect the horse's legs with travelling boots, or bandages and gamgee, against knocks, kicks and scrapes; also a tail bandage or guard, particularly in a lorry when the unprotected dock may be rubbed raw.

It is now illegal to travel shod horses in a trailer without a partition (but you *can* travel *un*shod horses without one): this could present problems for those horses which find it difficult to travel partitioned off; this usually happens because they feel a solid partition doesn't give them enough room to stand with their hindlegs sufficiently wide apart to balance themselves. However, the design of all new trailers will help because a part, or all of the partition consists of a hanging 'rubber skin' – though how deep this is does vary: it may be the whole thing, suspended from a bar which runs back from the breast-bar; or just the bottom 12in (30cm) or so. Note, too, that if the container on your lorry is more than 12ft (3.6m), horses must not be travelled loose as was the practice before, but must be partitioned individually.

On a long journey horses become easily dehydrated, so keep offering water (every 2–3 hours) and give them electrolytes; take a container of your own water, too, since a fussy horse may refuse to drink different water. Give a bran mash before leaving, and keep the feeds light and regular (every 3–4 hours), adding a little bran to each as the horse will be standing still for a long time, and if you can keep his bowels moving then his legs will not fill up so much. Colic is always a possibility so take some sort of relaxant and pain-killer, just in case.

## RAMPS

With all types of ramp every care must be taken to avoid unnecessary accidents; in the past there have been many, from ramps coming down unexpectedly quickly to people slipping and falling under them. Some ramps are so heavy it takes two people to handle them: beware of these when letting them down; children in particular should be kept well clear of all ramps and any loading operation. Never stand directly under a ramp if it can possibly be avoided; though unfortunately some ramps have only a centre handle, and sometimes only a centre catchment.

All hinges and fittings should be kept clean and well oiled; this also applies to internal fittings and partitions. The lorry should be cleaned or washed thoroughly all through after every trip, and if strange horses have been transported it should be disinfected.

# TRANSPORT OVERSEAS

Australian transport is very similar to that in England, though one of the most important concerns down under is in keeping a reasonable temperature for the horses whilst in transit. It is not unusual to have open-topped lorries, or just a canvas sheet over the roof, in order to keep the animals as cool and as comfortable as possible. In the more upmarket lorries, air conditioning is installed.

The USA largely uses trailers, of many different types and usually made of steel and aluminium; many are beautifully made and finished. In general abroad, trailers are widely used in the transportation of all horses. Also, horses are expected to travel very long distances and so tend to accept travelling far more readily than horses in the UK.

# INTERNATIONAL TRAVEL

With international travel companies, horses can be shipped and flown anywhere in the world, but there is always a risk of them panicking on the sea and in the air. Some may become dehydrated; others refuse to eat or drink; and colic both during and after travel is not uncommon. Some bad travellers even go to the point of throwing themselves on the floor. There are, however, always top-class travelling grooms plus a veterinary surgeon present. Many of the top firms supply all the necessary travelling gear, ie rugs, boots etc, but many, especially for air travel, do not like anything on the horse at all because of the risk of something coming undone and causing an accident. Pedens International is one of the leading horse transporters; John Parker International Ltd is another.

# INDEX

ACCESS *See* Approach
Alfa A, 80
Alfalfa, 84
Allergic reactions, bedding, 27, 28
All-weather surfaces, 124–5
American
  barn system, 17
  internal system, 15
  shelter and paddock, 48
  style complex, 12
  transport, 147
Anti-sweat rug, 74
Approach
  field shelter, 46
  water supply, 49
Atherstone girth, 66
Aubiose, 29
Australian
  fencing, 43
  field shelter, 46–7
  protection sheet/outdoor rug, 70, 71
  transport, 147
Automatic water bowls, 17, 22


BANDAGES, 69
  for travelling, 142
  knee injuries, 132
Barley, 80, 83
  straw, 27
Barn conversion, 17
Barrows, 24, 25, 35
Bedding, 20
  management, 30–3
  materials, 26–9
Big knee, 132
Biting, 15, 18
Bitless bridles, 62
Bits, 60–1
Blanket clip, 104, 105
Blankets *see* Rugs
Bolts, 19
Boots, 67–8, 114, 142
'Box walking', 18
Bran, 80, 82, 135, 145
Brick
  built stables, 11
  floor, 15
Bridles, 57–62, 114, 143
  storage, 56
Brushing boots, 67, 114
Bucket watering, 22, 49
Bulk feed, 19–20, 78, 80, 86
Burning, waste materials, 23, 34

CALCIUM IN SOIL, 38
Capped hocks, 26
Cavesson noseband, 57
Chaff, 80, 84
Chains
  door, 17
  tying with, 143
Charts, feeding, 80
Chewing, 14
  prevention, 12, 13, 18, 21, 41
Cleaning
  out, 32–3, 35, 36
  tack, 56
Clippers, 98
Clipping, 98–105
  procedures, 99–102
  styles, 103–5
Clothing
  fly fringes, 75
  hoods, 75, 133
  horse, 55, 70–6
  protective, for travel, 142, 145
  rugs, 70–4
  storage, 76
Coarse mix, 81
Cobs, schooling, 123
Cod-liver oil, 80, 84
Cold
  hosing, knee injuries, 132
  shoeing, 137
Colic, 79, 128, 145
Competition horses, feeding, 90
Concentrates, feed, 78, 80, 81–5
Concrete flooring, 10, 16
Condition, 88–9, 90
Construction, loose boxes, 10–11, 14
Cottage Craft girth, 66
Cotton summer sheets, 72
Coughs, 86
Creosoting, 13, 30, 41
Crib-biting, 18, 41
Cubes, feeding, 80, 81


DAY LIVING ACCOMMODATION, 11
Deep-litter beds, 30–1
Dental checks, 128
Design, stables, 11–17
  *see also* Layout
Doors, 18–19
Double bridle, 59
Double-gate system, 45
Drainage, 10, 16, 23, 38
  bed, 27, 31

Draughts, 17
Draw-reins, 124
Dressage
  girth, 66
  saddle, 64
Drinking supply, 17, 22, 49, 79
  travelling, 145


ELECTRIC FENCING, 41, 42, 43, 44
Electric groomer, 92
Empty stables, 23
Epsom salts, 128
Exercise, 18
  hoods, 75
  paddock, 12
  rug, 74
  saddle, 114
Exercising, 114–26
  free exercise, 126
  hill work, 119
  jumping, 120
  leading off, 118
  roadwork and hacking out, 116–17,
    136
  schooling, 121–5
  tack for, 114
Eye inspection, 128


FARRIERS, 135, 136, 137
Fastenings, gates, 45
Feed
  blocks, 50, 87
  bulk, 19–20, 78, 80, 86
  charts, 80
  concentrates, 78, 80, 81–5
  forage, 19–20, 86
  making up, 85
  storage, 85
Feeding, 78–90
  appliances, 19–21
  competition horses, 90
  in field, 39, 50, 87–9
  travelling, 145
Feet, care of, 31, 82, 95, 134–8
Fencing, 40–4
Fields, 38–52
  feeding in, 39, 50, 87–9
  fencing, 40–4
  gates, 45
  maintenance, 45, 51–2
  shelters, 46–8
  water supply, 49

Field shelters, 46–8
Fire, 23, 29, 34
Fitments, 17, 18–22, 86
Flash noseband, 58, 114
Flooring, 16
    brick, 15
    concrete, 10, 16
    rubber, 10, 16, 29
Fly fringes, 75
Forage, 19–20, 86
Foreleg, holding up of, 130
Free exercise, 126

GATES, 45
General purpose saddle, 64
Girths, 66
Grackle noseband, 58, 114
Grass, 79, 128
Grilles, 18
Grooming, 92–7
    equipment, 93
    feet, care of, 95
    heels, trimming, 96
    quarter marks, 95
    washing, 95, 96–7

HACKAMORE, 62
Hacking out, 116–17
Hacks, schooling, 122–3
Halters, 63
Hay, 80, 86
    racks, 17, 19, 86
Haylage, 86
Haynets, 19, 20, 86
Headcollars, 45, 63, 142
Heart rate, 129
Hedges
    as windbreaks, 40
    jumping, 120
    stock-proof, 42
Heels
    over-reach boots, 67
    trimming, 96
High tensile wire, 44
Hill work, 119
Hock boots, 142
Hocks, capped, 26
Hogging, mane, 102
Hoods, 75, 133
Hoof oil, 95
Hooves, care of, 31, 82, 95, 134–8
Horseboxes, 141
Horse clothing see Clothing, horse
Hosepipes, 23, 25
Hunter clip, 105
Hunters, schooling, 123

INDOOR SCHOOL, 125
In-hand bridles, 62
Injuries, leg, 26, 132–3
Insulux rug, 72, 73
Internal stabling, 10, 15

International travel, 147
Isolation
    box, 10
    stable, 46

JUMPING, 120
    saddle, 64

KAOLIN PASTE, Foreleg injury, 133
Kick-over bolts, 19
Knee
    boots, 68, 114, 142
    injuries, 132

LAMENESS, Recognition of, 131
Laminitis, 79, 131
Lawn mowings, 79
Layout, stable, 10
    see also Design
Leading off, 118
Lead-ropes, 63
Leg injuries, 26, 132–3
Lighting, 15, 125
Limestone soil, 38
Linseed, 80
Living out
    feeding, 39, 50, 87–9
    grooming, 92
    water supply, 49
Loading for travelling, 143–4
Loddon conversion, 14
Lonsdale girth, 66
Loose boxes
    American-style complex, 12
    measurements, 10–11
    portable, 30
    windows, 17
    wooden, 10–11, 14
Lorries, 140, 141

MANE
    hogging, 102
    plaiting, 108–10
    pulling, 106
    washing, 107
Mangers, 21
Martingales, 57, 58, 114, 120, 144
Masta rug, 70
Materials, stabling, 10
Measurements
    doorways, 18
    loose boxes, 10–11
    stalls, 16
Mineral licks, 31, 50, 84, 87
Mix, 80, 81
Mounting blocks, 24
Mucking out, 32–3, 35
    safety points, 36
Muck management, 23, 34
Mud fever, 17, 132

NAIL CLENCHES, Risen, 136
New Zealand rug, 70–1
Nosebands, 57, 58, 114
Numnah, 64, 114
    storage, 56
Nursing sick horses, 131
Nuts, 80, 81
Nylon string girth, 66

OAT STRAW, 27
Oats, 80, 83
Outdoor
    feeding, 39, 50, 87–9
    rugs, 70–1
Over-reach boots, 67
Overseas transport, 147

PAPER, Bedding, 28–9, 34
Pasture maintenance, 51–2
Peat moss, 29
Pelham bridle, 59
Pig-netting wire, 42
Plaiting, mane and tail, 107–12
Portable
    loose boxes, 30
    mounting blocks, 24
    wooden stable block, 13
Post-and-rail fencing, 40, 41, 42
Poultice, bran, 82, 135
Protective
    clothing for travel, 142, 145
    sheet/outdoor rug, Australian, 70
Pulling, mane and tail, 106
Pulse, taking of, 129

QUARTER MARKS, 95

RABBIT BURROWS, 52
Railing, 41
Rain scald, 17
Ramps, 146
Respiration, checking of, 130
Riding horse, schooling, 123
Road exercise, 116–17, 136
Rubber
    flooring, 10
    matting, 16, 29
Rubbing, 133
Rugs, 70–4
    rubbing caused by, 133
    storage, 76
Running martingale, 57, 58

SADDLES, 64–5
    for exercising, 114
    general purpose, 64
    savers, 64
    storage, 56
Safety, 23, 24, 36
Sand as bedding, 31

Schooling, 121–5
  area, 124–5
Semi-deep litter bed, 30
Shavings, wood, 28, 30, 31, 34
Sheath, washing of, 95, 97
Sheep, grazing, 51
Shoeing, 134–8
  types of shoe, 138
Showing saddle, 64
Sliding doors, 14
Smoking, 23
Snaffle bridles, 57, 58, 114, 143
'Spelling', 12
Stable
  rugs, 72–3
  tools, 25
  yard, standards, 23, 24
Stabling, 10–36
  bedding, 20, 26–33
  cleaning out, 32–3, 35, 36
  design, 11–17
  fitments, 17, 18–22, 86
  internal, 10, 15
  muck management, 23, 34
  safety, 23, 24, 36
  standards, 23, 24
Stalls, 10, 16
Standing martingale, 58, 114, 120, 144
Steel pen, 49
Stock-horse saddle, 65
Stock-proof fence, 42
Storage
  bins, feed, 85
  rugs, 76
  tack, 56
Straw, 27, 30, 34
Stream as water supply, 49
Studs, 138
Sugar beet, 80, 83
Super Ted, 89
Supplements, 80, 84
Swollen limbs, 132, 145
Synthetic saddles, 65

TACK, 55, 56–69
  bandages, 69, 132, 142
  boots, 67–8, 114, 142
  bridles, 57–62, 114, 143
  cleaning, 56
  for exercising, 114
  for schooling cobs, 123
  girths, 66
  halters and lead-ropes, 63
  headcollars, 45, 63, 142
  room, 11
  saddles, 64–5
  storage, 56
Tail
  bandages, 142
  grooming, 95
  plaiting, 107, 111–12
  pulling, 106
  washing, 97
Tape and electrified wire, 44
Temperature
  and bedding, 31
  for horses in transit, 147
  of stabling, 10, 11, 12, 15
  taking horses', 130
Tendon boots, 68
Tetanus, 45, 130
Tools, stable, 25
Top-bolts, 19
Trace clip, 103, 104, 105
Trailers, 140–1
Transport, 140–7
  clothing for, 142, 145
  horseboxes, 141
  of horses together, 145
  loading, 143–4
  overseas, 147
  ramps, 146
  trailers, 140–1
  unloading, 145
Travelling horses together, 145
Troughs, 49
Turning out, stabled horses, 126

Turn-out rug, 70, 71
Twitch, use of, 102, 137

UNLOADING, TRAVELLING, 145

VACCINATIONS, 130
Ventilation, 17
Veterinary care
  basic health checks, 128–30
  lameness, 131
  leg injuries, 26, 132–3
  rubbing, 133
  shoeing and footcare, 31, 82, 95,
    134–8
Vices, 15, 18, 41

WASHING, 96–7
  mane, 107
  sheath, 95, 97
  tail, 97
Water, supply, 17, 22, 49, 79
  travelling, 145
Weaving, 15, 18
Western saddle, 65
'Westropp' petal boots, 67
Wheat straw, 27
Wheelbarrows see Barrows
White tape, fencing, 44
Wilson bit, 58
Windbreaks, 40
Windows, 17
Windsucking, 18
Wintering, 17
Wood shavings, 28, 30, 31, 34
Wooden
  loose boxes, 10-11, 14
  stable block, 13
Woollen rugs, 72, 74
Worm burden, pasture, 51
Worming, 130
Wurlyboot, 132

'YARDING', 17
Young horses, stabling, 11, 16

# EQUESTRIAN TITLES FROM DAVID & CHARLES

## BEHAVIOUR PROBLEMS IN HORSES

**Susan McBane**

Learn more about just what makes your horse 'tick' – and how a deeper understanding of his character can help you solve all kinds of behavioural problems.

## COMPETITION TRAINING For Horse and Rider

**Monty Mortimer**

An authoritative and comprehensive manual covering all aspects of training the competition horse and rider.

## DAVID BROOME'S TRAINING MANUAL

**Marcy Pavord**

Marcy Pavord takes an intimate look at David Broome's method of producing showjumping horses – from selecting and buying through to training novices, dealing with problems and competing at international level; and gives an insight into this famous rider's brilliant record.

## FITNESS FOR HORSE AND RIDER

**Jane Holderness-Roddam**

Follow the advice given in this excellent, highly illustrated manual, and learn how to increase your enjoyment and satisfaction from this popular sport.

## FROM FOAL TO FULL-GROWN

**Janet Lorch**

This excellent, down-to-earth guide provides invaluable practical advice for the single mare owner or inexperienced breeder.

## HORSE BREEDING

**Peter Rossdale**

This acclaimed work, first published in 1981 and now extensively revised and updated, is acknowledged as the standard reference source in the equestrian world.

## HORSE CARE & RIDING A Thinking Approach

**Susan McBane**

Practical, down-to-earth, reliable and easy to follow, *Horse Care & Riding* is the ideal guide to looking after horses and ponies.

## THE HORSE OWNER'S HANDBOOK

**Monty Mortimer**

An ideal owner's manual that teaches the basics soundly, and will improve your understanding of how to keep your horse or pony safe, healthy, happy and useful. It dispels the myths surrounding stable management and horsemanship, and shows that keeping your own horse is simply commonsense.

## THE HORSE RIDER'S HANDBOOK

**Monty Mortimer**

Worth its weight in gold to every rider who takes the sport seriously, Monty Mortimer's handbook is complete in every way. He takes you through every stage of training from handling the foal to jumping and dressage. He explains the requirements of competitive riding, and how to achieve success.

## THE HORSE'S HEALTH FROM A–Z An Equine Veterinary Dictionary

**Peter Rossdale & Susan Wreford**

A fully revised and extended edition of this classic title, covering definitions of all veterinary terms relating to the horse, and now issued in paperback.

## THE ILLUSTRATED GUIDE TO HORSE TACK

**Susan McBane**

The definitive work on horse tack and equipment, with over 200 line illustrations and explanatory text on care and use of tack, and correct methods of fitting.

## KEEPING A HORSE OUTDOORS

**Susan McBane**

First published in 1984 and now completely updated, this excellent handbook covers everything the owner needs to know about keeping a horse or pony in its natural state.

## THE LESS-THAN-PERFECT RIDER Overcoming Common Riding Problems

**Lesley Bayley & Caroline Davis**

An excellent, straightforward guide which shows how any rider can improve his or her technique and become a better rider; and which will help nervous riders overcome their doubts and fears.

## LUNGEING The Horse & Rider

**Sheila Inderwick**

Written in a straightforward, practical style and illustrated with explanatory drawings, this step-by-step guide takes you from the basic principles and essential equipment to more advanced movements. There is also advice on using lungeing to train riders, and the emphasis throughout is on trainer technique.

## MARY THOMSON'S EVENTING YEAR A Month-by Month Plan for Training a Champion

**Debby Sly with Mary Thomson**

A fascinating month-by-month look at the life of the 1992 Mitsubishi Badminton Horse Trials Champion, following the training and progress of her world-class horses at novice, intermediate and advanced levels, in an Olympic year.

## PRACTICAL DRESSAGE

**Jane Kidd**

This clear, straightforward and extremely practical guide is essential reading for everyone who wants to understand and enjoy the sport to the full. Jane Kidd, a leading dressage writer and international competitor, reveals the basic principles, and gives helpful advice and guidance to riders of all ages.

## PRACTICAL EVENTING

**Jane Holderness-Roddam**

How to select, care for and train the event horse, with detailed advice on tackling cross-country courses, from a world-class competitor and author.

## PRACTICAL SHOWING

**Nigel Hollings**

Nigel Hollings shows the key to success is attention to every last detail. He freely gives away his 'tricks of the trade' in his winning combination of ringcraft, showmanship and knowing what the judge will be looking for.

## PRACTICAL SHOWJUMPING

**Peter Churchill**

Peter Churchill provides clear, comprehensive guidance on every aspect of showjumping, from the basic principles to the final preparations. He examines attitude, choosing the right horse, fitness, training, equipment, jumping technique, and riding the course, and there are over 80 photographs to illustrate and complement the text.

## THE RIDING INSTRUCTOR'S HANDBOOK

**Monty Mortimer**

A comprehensive manual for anyone involved in teaching others how to ride correctly and effectively.

## ROBERT SMITH'S YOUNG SHOWJUMPER
### Selecting, Training, Competing

**Rachel Lambert**

Advice from a top international rider on selecting and training your show-jumping horse up to competition level, with over 100 specially commissioned photographs.

## THE STABLE VETERINARY HANDBOOK

**Colin Vogel**

Here at last is a reliable and comprehensive handbook for horse owners who want to understand and treat their horse's less serious ailments themselves. It includes an essential first-aid kit for horse owners, and clear information on each type of problem.

## UNDERSTANDING HORSES
### The Key to Success

**Garda Langley**

Why do horses prefer those of their own colour? How can we motivate horses to do what we want? How can we re-train a horse that is reluctant to be caught? This in-depth study of horse psychology answers these and hundres of other such questions, and reveals what makes horses tick.